D0220067

FANTASY

Fantasy addresses a previously neglected area within film studies. This book looks at the key aesthetics, themes, debates and issues at work within this popular genre and examines films and franchises that illustrate these concerns. Contemporary case studies include:

- *Alice in Wonderland* (2010)
- *Avatar* (2009)
- *The Dark Knight* (2008)
- *Edward Scissorhands* (1990)
- *The Lord of the Rings* (2001–2003)
- *Pirates of the Caribbean* (2003–2007)
- *Prince of Persia: The Sands of Time* (2010)
- *Shrek* (2001)
- *Twelve Monkeys* (1995)

The authors also consider fantasy film and its relationship to myth, legend and fairy tale, examining its important role in contemporary culture. This book provides an historical overview of the genre, its influences and evolution, placing fantasy film within the socio-cultural contexts of production and consumption and with reference to relevant theory and critical debates.

This is the perfect introduction to the world of fantasy film and investigates the links between fantasy film and gender, race, psychoanalysis, technology, storytelling and spectacle, realism, adaptation, and time.

Jacqueline Furby is Senior Lecturer and Course Leader for Film at Southampton Solent University, UK.

Claire Hines is Senior Lecturer in Film and Television Studies at Southampton Solent University, UK.

Routledge Film Guidebooks

The Routledge Film Guidebooks offer a clear introduction to and overview of the work of key filmmakers, movements, or genres. Each guidebook contains an introduction, including a brief history; defining characteristics and major films; a chronology; key debates surrounding filmmakers, movements, or genres; and pivotal scenes, focusing on narrative structure, camerawork, and production quality.

Bollywood
Tejaswini Ganti

James Cameron
Alexandra Keller

Jane Campion
Deb Verhoeven

Horror
Brigid Cherry

Film Noir
Jennifer Fay and Justus Nieland

Documentary
Dave Saunders

Romantic Comedy
Claire Mortimer

Westerns
John White

Fantasy
Jacqueline Furby and Claire Hines

FANTASY

JACQUELINE FURBY AND CLAIRE HINES

Routledge
Taylor & Francis Group

LONDON AND NEW YORK

First published 2012
by Routledge
2 Park Square, Milton Park, Abingdon, Oxon OX14 4RN

Simultaneously published in the USA and Canada
by Routledge
711 Third Avenue, New York, NY 10017

Routledge is an imprint of the Taylor & Francis Group, an informa business

© 2012 Jacqueline Furby and Claire Hines

The right of Jacqueline Furby and Claire Hines to be identified as
authors of this work has been asserted by them in accordance with
sections 77 and 78 of the Copyright, Designs and Patents Act 1988.

All rights reserved. No part of this book may be reprinted or
reproduced or utilised in any form or by any electronic, mechanical,
or other means, now known or hereafter invented, including
photocopying and recording, or in any information storage or
retrieval system, without permission in writing from the publishers.

Trademark notice: Product or corporate names may be trademarks or
registered trademarks, and are used only for identification and
explanation without intent to infringe.

British Library Cataloguing in Publication Data
A catalogue record for this book is available from the British Library

Library of Congress Cataloging in Publication Data
Furby, Jacqueline.
Fantasy / Jacqueline Furby and Claire Hines.
     p. cm. – (Routledge film guidebooks)
   Includes bibliographical references and index.
   Includes filmography.
   1. Fantasy films–History and criticism. I. Hines, Claire. II. Title.
PN1995.9.F36F86 2011
791.43′615--dc22   2011009247

ISBN: 978–0–415–48687–3 (hbk)
ISBN: 978–0–415–48688–0 (pbk)
ISBN: 978–0–203–80445–2 (ebk)

Typeset in Joanna by
Swales & Willis Ltd, Exeter, Devon

MIX
Paper from
responsible sources
FSC® C004839
www.fsc.org

Printed and bound in Great Britain by
TJ International Ltd, Padstow, Cornwall

This book is dedicated to our teachers,
our students, our friends and our families.

CONTENTS

LIST OF ILLUSTRATIONS

FIGURES

TABLES

ACKNOWLEDGEMENTS

Special thanks go to our families and friends for putting up with us while we worked on this book and for not complaining when there were long gaps between visits. We also owe thanks to Southampton Solent University for a grant of money in support of this project in 2009–10. Thank you to our colleagues past and present in the Film & Television programme at Southampton Solent University for support and encouragement. And we thank the readers of our original proposal for their valuable comments. Finally many thanks to Aileen Storry at Routledge for her continued patience and support and for having exactly the right name to commission a book on fantasy.

We are grateful to Routledge for kindly giving permission to reproduce the diagram of the 'paraxial' from Rosemary Jackson (1981) *Fantasy: The Literature of Subversion*, p. 19.

1

FANTASY STORYTELLING AND FILM

Fantasy pervades human culture, that is, fantasy pervades humanity.

(Collins and Pearce 1985: 4)

The question of fantasy . . . helps to explain the fascination, and so the power, of cinema.

(Donald 1989: 7)

We all indulge in fantasy of some kind. As human beings we are distinguished by our ability to imagine, to dream, to wish for things, and to make-believe scenarios, events and stories that extend far beyond our everyday experience, and to 'enter worlds of infinite possibility' (Matthews 2002: 1). Fantasy film is just over one hundred years old, but the tradition of storytelling is rich and ancient. Fantasy is the oldest form of fiction, found in cultures across the world, and has remained a chief fictional mode in the late twentieth and early twenty-first century. If, as Robert Collins and Howard Pearce state in the quote above, 'fantasy pervades humanity', then surely understanding fantasy film, now one of our favourite ways of telling stories, is a route to understanding what it means to be human.

Yet despite this undoubted longevity, popularity and significance – in the foreword to the updated edition of Susan Napier's book on anime she even refers to a recent 'global hunger for fantasy' (2005: xi) – fantasy often suffers from an unflattering reputation at the hands of critics. Indeed fantasy is typically criticized for being the lowbrow, popular, pulp, childish and lightweight poor relation of more highbrow, grownup and serious forms based on the realist (mimetic) arts. Certainly, until the current upsurge of interest in fantasy film there have been very few full-length academic studies on this popular genre. This is surprising considering that the subject of fantasy is central to film production and consumption in a number of ways. Thematically, for example, fantasy is at the heart of the majority of the stories told in cinema; stylistically, fantasy dominates film's symbolic *mise-en-scène*, and ideologically, fantasy fulfils real and important social and cultural functions for both filmmakers and audiences. A number of individual films have received attention, such as *The Wizard of Oz* (1939), *It's a Wonderful Life* (1947), and *The Lord of the Rings* trilogy (2001–2003), but the fantasy genre as a whole is more often than not overlooked in preference of its fantastic relations science fiction and horror.

Therefore, in this book we focus on the world of fantasy film, and give an introduction to the theoretical, historical and contextual approaches to its study. Our coverage of fantasy film is necessarily selective. The areas taken into account reflect our own interests in fantasy and what we hope will appeal to our twenty-first century reader. The fact that 'Genre studies has historically been dominated by analysis of the major Hollywood genres' (Langford 2005: x) means that Hollywood is our main concern, though in the past fantasy has not been counted among those principal genres. Our choices attempt to redress the problem of a lack of critical regard for mainstream fantasy film, and this is another reason we wish to concentrate mainly though not exclusively on Hollywood fantasy. Whilst this rules out an in-depth discussion of other national cinemas and fantasy traditions, we nonetheless recognize the fundamental importance of non-Hollywood and non-English language fantasy forms and international contexts, and where relevant we will consider the influence of other cinemas and alternative filmmaking styles.

This current chapter discusses the roots and pre-filmic history of fantasy (in oral folk tradition, fairy tales and myths), explores the functions of fantasy, and suggests some ways to go about solving the problem of defining the fantasy film genre. Chapter 2 introduces some theoretical approaches to, and critical debates on, fantasy. Chapter 3 includes an account of the technological evolution and development of fantasy film's social, historical and industrial frameworks. Finally, in Chapter 4 we use contemporary case studies to explore specific fantasy films in relation to key cultural, thematic and theoretical concerns. The overall aim of this guidebook is to at least in part find ways to support James Donald's claim, cited at the beginning of this chapter, that the 'question of fantasy . . . helps to explain the fascination, and so the power, of cinema'.

FANTASY (TAP)ROOTS AND STORY OCEANS

Fantasy film is a popular medium through which we tell our stories to one another today. The act of telling one another stories has as its heritage the magical mythic tales, folklore and legends that people have exchanged all over the world, both before and since the first recorded Sumerian (roughly present-day Iraq) fantasy *The Epic of Gilgamesh* from the second millennium BCE (Before the Current Era). The ancestral roots of contemporary fantasy film can therefore be traced back to earlier forms of fictional storytelling such as the novel, short story, epic and lyric poetry, literary fairy tale, romance, oral folktale, myth, and legend. Though fantasy film may differ in some ways from these literary and non-literary forms, it is evident that they share many things in common including themes, characters, archetypes, subjects, structure, plot lines and stories.

Obvious examples of stories that constitute part of what John Clute and John Grant, in their exhaustive encyclopaedia of fantasy, call 'the ocean that is the literature of the fantastic' (1997: vii), include many varieties of English literature now adapted for film. For instance, J.R.R. Tolkien's hugely influential high fantasy novels *The Lord of the Rings* (1954–5) and *The Hobbit* (1937), which heralded a resurgence of fantasy in England, and C.S. Lewis's *The Chronicles of Narnia*, from *The Lion, the Witch and the Wardrobe* (1950) to *The Last Battle* (1956). The publication of *The Lord of the Rings* changed the face of the literary fantasy world and ignited the imagination of generations of devoted readers. In *The Lord of the Rings: The Mythology of Power*, Jane Chance writes that what partly accounts for the success of Tolkien's masterpiece is that it offered a 'twentieth-century understanding of the nature of good and evil, the value of community, the natural order of the universe, and the singularity of the individual' (2001: 1). She adds that in this 'fantasy of the empowerment of the individual, Tolkien . . . most captivated a modern world-audience' (Chance 2001: 1).

The themes mentioned by Chance are common concerns of fantasy-related fiction throughout history, though some may occasionally get turned upside-down. For example, in the works of Gothic authors, such as Mervyn Peake's *Gormenghast* (1950), Bram Stoker's *Dracula* (1897), *Frankenstein; or, The Modern Prometheus* by Mary Shelley (1818), and the eighteenth-century writer Horace Walpole's *The Castle of Otranto* (1764), often described as the first gothic novel (see Jackson 1998: 95). Gothic literature is fascinated by boundaries – between good and evil; light and dark; life and death – and possesses a dark eroticism where strangely attractive and compelling characters hint at repressed violence and perverse pleasures. This form is typified by Edgar Allan Poe's short stories: *The Fall of the House of Usher* (1839), *The Pit and the Pendulum* (1842), and *The Masque of the Red Death* (1842). Poe's gothic tales, adapted for film by B-movie director Roger Corman in the 1960s, occupy the dark boundary between fantasy and horror as they allude to uncanny, mysterious events in a world that looks very like our own. Such stories are constructed so that it is left in doubt whether the mysterious, sinister or supernatural events that take place should be understood as real or simply the fantastical product of a fevered (or perhaps intoxicated) imagination.

The distinction between what might be considered realistic and fantastic only acquired meaning during the scientific revolution in sixteenth- and seventeenth-century Western Europe. Previously, as Clute and Grant note:

> most Western literature contained huge amounts of material 20th-century readers would think of as fantastical. It is, however, no simple matter to determine the degree to which various early writers distinguished, before the rise of science, between what we would call fantastical and what we would call realistic.
>
> (1997: 338)

For this reason it is problematic to assume that those writing what we now know as fantasy always understood their work to 'deliberately confront or contradict the "real"' (Clute and Grant 1997: 338). Fantasy clearly existed before 1600, but as Clute and Grant explain: 'it is quite something else to suggest that the perceived impossibility of these stories *was their point*' (1997: 338, emphasis in original). Though we ought not to take for granted that a previous age thought of fantasy in the same way that we do, and despite the difficulty of labelling writing prior to the mid-eighteenth century as fantasy, there is an 'ocean of story' (Clute and Grant 1997: 704) that modern fantasy filmmakers draw from.

Prior to the epistemic break of the scientific revolution, which eventually fostered the emergence of writing grounded in literary realism such as the novel and short story, there were some memorable celebrations of fancy, myth and romance, labelled 'taproot texts' by Clute and Grant (1997: 921). The taproot text is influential writing which existed 'before those we can legitimately call fantasy' (Clute and Grant 1997: 921), yet cannot for reasons of influence or quality be excluded from a discussion of the fantastic. In these constructions of alternative, supernatural realms, heroes, anti-heroes, sorcerers and other fantastic creatures do battle. Typical Renaissance English language fantasy taproots include John Milton's epic poems *Paradise Lost* (1667) and *Paradise Regained* (1671), William Shakespeare's plays *The Tempest* (c.1610) and *A Midsummer Night's Dream* (c.1596), and Edmund Spenser's allegorical poem *The Faerie Queene* (1596). Of these only Shakespeare's plays have enjoyed much popularity as film adaptations, but they more than make up for the lack of attention to other Renaissance works. *The Tempest* and *A Midsummer Night's Dream* have a great many films to their credit, the most recent being *A Midsummer Night's Dream* (1999) and *The Tempest* (2011).

Earlier examples of important taproot texts written in English include Sir Thomas Mallory's romance *Le Morte d'Arthur* (1485) from the late Middle Ages, which drew on the literature and legends of Britain and Europe to tell the story of King Arthur and the Knights of the Round Table, and has since fostered numerous fantasy films, such as *Excalibur* (1981). Geoffrey Chaucer's *The Canterbury Tales* (c.1400) also brought together a wide variety of stories from a range of sources, including *The Bible*, Arthurian legend, Greek and Roman mythology, medieval mystery plays, and fable, and put them into the mouths of a group of pilgrims travelling from London to Canterbury. Centuries later

Chaucer is one of the central characters in the postmodern film *A Knight's Tale* (2001), which takes inspiration from *The Canterbury Tales* and anachronistically mixes modern-day attitudes with a story that borrows from medieval romance.

Sir Gawain and the Green Knight, by an unknown author in the late fourteenth century, is another heroic adventure based on Arthurian legend, German and Celtic folklore, in which one of the Knights of the Round Table is tested for his adherence to the laws of chivalry and courtly love. On screen Gawain's tale is seen in the 1984 fantasy film *Sword of the Valiant: The Legend of Gawain and the Green Knight*. And modern cinema audiences might also recognize the epic Anglo-Saxon poem *Beowulf* (c.800) in its twenty-first century animated incarnation, *Beowulf* (2007). Clearly this inheritance of English literature is but one drop in the vast ocean of fantasy story which includes many others from many other nations and languages, and cultures from around the world, often proving to be both deeply influential and enduring.

TRADITIONAL FORMS: MYTH, LEGEND AND FAIRY TALE

Having considered some of the stories that provide the ancestry of modern fantasy, we can identify the key forms through which these (tap)root tales find their way to us in film. These forms – myth, legend and fairy tale – are distinguished by their purpose, audience, makers and relationship to the real world.

Myths are understood to be a fundamental genre of symbolic, sacred narratives which explain the birth and workings of the cosmos, and generally describe events in the very distant (primordial) past (see Eliade 1963). Myth is concerned with (supernatural) gods and their actions, and how it is through their 'intervention that man [sic] himself is what he is today, a mortal, sexed, and cultural being' (Eliade 1963: 6). Myths set out codes of behaviour, systems of belief and morality, justify actions and ways of doing things, and 'support the stability and functioning of whole societies' (Haase 2008: 653). Examples of myths might include well-known stories from *The Bible*, the Indian *Rig Veda*, Greek and Roman mythology, Celtic tales such as those of Cuchulain, and stories of Germanic, Old Norse and Icelandic heroes.

The term 'myth' popularly carries the meaning of invention or fiction, yet as Donald Haase notes, 'Folklorists see myths as stories about grand events in ancient times, often discussing the origin of the present world' (2008: 652). Myths are therefore 'held to be true in the culture where they belong' (Haase 2008: 652), and thought to be based on real (pre)histories of the deeds of the gods, whereas legends are similarly 'true' stories but about human deeds (rather than deeds of deities) that have actually happened at some time in the real historical past. Haase says that 'Legends discuss human encounters with the supernatural power in the present world' (2008: 653). Familiar legends include tales of the exploits of Robin Hood from Nottingham, or stories that recount the founding of Rome by Romulus and Remus. Despite having been written over 2,000 years ago, mythological and legendary tales such as those of the Trojan horse, the heroic deeds of Achilles, Ulysses, and Hector, and the beauty of Helen of Troy are still very popular with contemporary filmmakers and cinema audiences. Myths and legends of the ancient Greco-Roman world, including Virgil's *Aeneid* (29–19 BCE) and Homer's *Iliad* and the *Odyssey* (800 BCE), inspire Hollywood films such as *Troy* (2004), *Clash of the Titans* (2010), and *Percy Jackson and the Olympians: The Lightning Thief* (2010).

While myth and legend are believed to have been at one time real it is usually safe to consider that fairy tales tell of fictional events. Fairy tale is the English term for a literary short story (rather than an oral folktale), which typically features characters from folklore such as witches, goblins, fairies, giants and elves involved in magical or enchanted happenings. They are 'fictional . . . narratives whose events take place in a fantasy world that is regarded as unreal by the teller and audience' (Haase 2008: 653). The fairy tale is a significant form of fictional storytelling which (like myth and legend) is probably familiar to all societies; it is known in French as *conte de fée*, in Italian as *fiaba*, in German as *Märchen*, and in Swedish as *folksaga* (Ziolkowski 2009: 46). So widespread is the form that Marina Warner describes the fairy tale as 'promiscuous and omnivorous and anarchically heterogeneous' (1995: xvii). Fairy tales are generally agreed to be the written or literary versions of earlier oral folktales, though not all fairy tales can be traced back to the oral tradition (see Zipes 2000).

Folklorist Jack Zipes notes that the oral tales, on which many of these literary fairy tales were based, are 'thousands of years old' and whilst he says that 'it is impossible to date and explain how they were generated', he argues that they would have formed part of the tools for survival and adaptation to changing environmental conditions, used by their tellers and audiences (2006b: 13). Zipes says that we know from 'archaeological evidence such as cave paintings, pottery, tombs, parchments, manuscripts, and scrolls that tales with fantastic creatures, magical transformation, and wondrous events were told and disseminated in tribes, groups, communities, and societies' (2006b: 13). Those tales that spoke of matters that remained important to a culture survived and were passed on, especially those that had ties to rites of passage or ritual 'such as birth, marriage, death, harvest, initiation, and so on'(Zipes 2006b: 13).

Long after, the surviving tales were collected together and set into print as relics of our early human dependency on stories of wonder, fantasy and magic. The fairy tale form was nurtured in the middle of the seventeenth century in the salons of aristocratic Parisienne women, though earlier models of the literary fairy tale tradition were provided by two Italian writers, Giovanni Francesco Straparola and Giambattista Basile. Contemporary readers of fairy tale fantasy may be more familiar with the versions collected by Charles Perrault (c.1695), the Brothers Grimm (1812), or Hans Christian Andersen (1835–7), though viewers asked to name stories in the classical fairy tale canon would no doubt cite those adapted by Disney, such as *Snow White and the Seven Dwarfs* (1937), *Cinderella* (1949), *Sleeping Beauty* (1958), *The Little Mermaid* (1989) and *Beauty and the Beast* (1991).

The three key genres of myth, legend and fairy tale are closely connected and their boundaries are often indistinct. Haase says that 'Many fairy-tale motifs, such as the fight with the dragon or a trip to the other world derive historically from myths' (2008: 653). Not only have fairy tales been freely adapted, but the characters and creatures, the settings, the iconography, the themes, and the narrative structure have all migrated to fantasy film. Writing on myths and fairy tales Mircea Eliade says that the structure common to these traditional story forms, which should be familiar to fantasy film viewers as well, is: (1) initiatory ordeal, (2) journey and (3) marriage (1963: 201). These initiatory ordeals may be 'battles with the monster, apparently insur-mountable obstacles, [and] riddles to be solved, impossible tasks' (Eliade

1963: 201). In these tales Eliade says that we also find some variation on 'the descent to Hades [underworld or hell] or the ascent to Heaven (or . . . death and resurrection)', and finally 'marrying the princess' (1963: 201).

Jan De Vries stresses that this common 'coming of age' structure can be understood as representing the hero's journey (in Eliade's words) from 'ignorance and immaturity to the spiritual age of the adult' (Eliade 1963: 201). George Lucas's 1977 film *Star Wars* follows the 'coming of age' structure, but we can also find this pattern being repeated in other popular fantasy films like the *Harry Potter* series (2001–2011), as well as many other genres. The coming of age story continues to be relevant to societies today; we still benefit from the imaginary initiation supplied by these tales that speak of the lives of all people 'made up of an unbroken series of "ordeals," "death," and "resurrections"' (Eliade 1963: 202).

So fantasy comes to us through myth, legend and fairy tale, through stories of epic adventure, romance, magic and transformation of every age. It has even been suggested that we find the ancestry of fantasy perhaps as far back as the Upper Palaeolithic period, 40,000 years ago, but certainly in cave paintings such as those found at Lascaux in France dating from around 14,000 BCE. The paintings represent imagined scenes of hunting, ritual, ceremony and, possibly, mythology. Proof of the human urge to make and receive fantastical tales appears to be universal, evidenced wherever there is a language and medium of storytelling, giving form to Tolkien's view that 'to ask what is the origin of stories . . . is to ask what is the origin of language and of the mind' (1966: 44).

Considering this long history, there is something enchanting about the idea that fantasy is a portal through which we can connect to human lives and endeavour back through the modern era, back through the break caused by the birth of the pragmatic, scientific age, back through the dark ages, and beyond. This journey through time is enabled by a way of considering the world, a mythic, magical, and romantic view that there is actually more to life than can be explained away by science and reason. This might suggest that fantastic forms have existed (even though they may be called other things) throughout human history, but what causes this longevity, the persistence of fantasy storytelling?

WHY WE NEED FANTASY AND WHY WE TELL FANTASY STORIES

In *The Science of Discworld II: The Globe* human beings are referred to as 'the storytelling ape' (Pratchett *et al.* 2002: 325). Fantasy novelist Terry Pratchett and his co-authors say that 'what makes humans different from all other creatures . . . is not language, or mathematics, or science. It is not religion, or art, or politics, either. All of those things are mere side effects of the invention of story' (2002: 325). The authors summarize the continued importance of storytelling by saying that 'we still use stories to run our lives' (Pratchett *et al.* 2002: 325). As well as the roles of guidance, motivation and education implied by this idea, fantasy storytelling also appeals to our emotions, and as David Pringle notes fantasy often 'deals in the fulfilment of desire . . . in the sense of the yearning of the human heart for a kinder world, a better self, a wholer experience, a sense of truly belonging' (1998: 8). These utopian impulses are related to what Christopher Booker describes as 'our ability to "imagine", to bring up to our conscious perception the images of things which are not actually in front of our eyes' (2004: 3). This capacity enables us to feed our appetite for storytelling when awake, and our need to dream scenarios when asleep.

Fantasy storytelling transports us, as Pringle says, 'into new realms of imaginative (im)possibility' and can provide us with 'heartfelt delights' (1998: 19). Richard Davis comments that because we inhabit:

> a world in which we often have so little control over what happens to us . . . our culture has become positively obsessed with the idea of transcending the confines of this world for the cool fresh air of another. Whether it's by a red pill, a secret wardrobe, a looking glass, or a rabbit-hole, it doesn't really matter. We'll take it.
>
> (2010: 1)

This view of fantasy as escapism is often seen as a bad thing by critics who denigrate it for being 'trivial' and having no 'serious' benefit, though Clute and Grant point out that escapism is 'a term that more accurately describes the motives of the reader than the nature of what is read' (1997: 321).

The potential for escape, emancipation and individual agency offered by fantasy's imaginative terrain can only ever be temporary as we go back to our own world at the end of the film. And as an ideological or political concept escapism certainly carries a negative connotation: that to escape is to turn away from something we ought rather to be attending to. Some critics argue that providing people with a temporary escape prevents them from making permanent changes to the conditions of their lives (such as poverty, pain, sorrow, or injustice) from which they wish to flee (see Dyer 2002). Obviously escapism is an important function available to the fantasy film audience, but also surely one of the pleasures of reading a novel, or poetry, watching a play or attending an art exhibition too. And modern life is unquestionably busy enough that we should not have to justify or feel guilty about spending a relatively short time, and some money, on such leisure pursuits. Furthermore, escape need not necessarily imply passivity or intellectual inactivity. After all someone who enters into an imagined world may return from it having gained insights into their own, real world and may therefore be newly equipped to make material changes to their lives.

Far from being superficial and worthless, fantasy storytelling might serve a number of real, significant, valuable, though by no means unproblematic roles. Zipes returns repeatedly to the fundamental importance that traditional storytelling forms have held for us throughout human history. Indeed he begins his book *Fairy Tales and the Art of Subversion* by saying that 'the fairy tale may be the most important cultural and social event in most children's lives' (Zipes 2006a: 1). It follows that some makers of oral folk and literary fairy tales created them specifically to perform the task of preparing young people for the 'roles that they idealistically believed they should play in society' (Zipes 2006a: 30) and adult life. This didactic tendency has raised questions and divided opinions about the desirability of using children's fantasy as effective teaching aids, or persuasive tools of indoctrination, depending on which viewpoint is favoured. For instance, in the 1960s, critics of the Brothers Grimm's early nineteenth-century fairy tales accused them of promoting sexism and racism, which 'served a socialization process that placed great emphasis on passivity, industry and self-sacrifice for girls, and on activity, competition, and accumulation of wealth for boys' (Zipes 2006a: 60). We should not then underestimate the impact these tales (whether in literary or film form) have on their readers or viewers. Some critics argue however that whilst film clearly has the potential to speak of the social-cultural moment, and to provide a lens through which to view it, fantasy does not make it easy for us to recognize problems such as social inequalities or the part that film might play to uphold and even strengthen them.

In *Framing Monsters: Fantasy Film and Social Alienation* Joshua Bellin discusses the role of fantasy film in 'circulating and validating pernicious cultural beliefs embedded within specific social settings' (2005: 2). Bellin names *King Kong* (1933), *The Wizard of Oz*, the *Sinbad* trilogy (1958, 1973, 1977) and *Twelve Monkeys* (1995) as the kind of fantasy films which, he says, insidiously identify 'marginalized social groups as monstrous threats to the dominant social order' (2005: 2). Bellin asserts that:

> fantasy films *frame* social reality: they provoke a perspective, provide a context, produce a way of seeing. As such, if these function as mass-cultural rituals that give image to historically determinate anxieties, wishes, and needs, they simultaneously function by stimulating, endorsing, and broadcasting the very anxieties, wishes, and needs to which they give image.
>
> (2005: 9, emphasis in original)

Of course, the economic imperative of the commercial film industry means that its filmmakers must take the majority audience's aspirations, beliefs, prejudices and ideologies into account. This can lead to the tension in fantasy storytelling between what Warner calls 'acquiescence . . . and rebellion' (1995: 409).

It would seem reasonable to assume that tales that are canonical to a society will normally be those that have been approved because they reinforce established belief and power systems, though Zipes (2006b) argues that not all canonical tales do this job of reinforcement. 'Indeed', he says, 'there are thousands if not millions of tales that people tell time and again . . . that bring people together and expose the contradictions of the powerful and suggest ways in which the oppressed can survive' (Zipes 2006b: 229). In the end, he notes, 'tradition always engenders subversion in a dialectical process' (Zipes 2006b: 229). To illustrate he offers the instance of Robin Hood, one of a number of legends that 'question the authoritarianism of authority figures. Robin Hood takes from the rich and gives to the poor and tries to pave the way for a just ruler in England' (Zipes 2006b: 229). Perhaps a story need only 'offer a way of putting questions' (Warner 1995: 411), and suggest that there is more than one way to see events, to be subversive. We might therefore propose that fantasy, which is structured around the notion of seeing familiar things differently, and by extension looking at the different with familiarity, is perfectly placed to ask questions about the nature of our reality.

Indeed, stories are a vital component in social change because in order to be able to achieve something you must first be able to imagine it. In addition to being the product of imagination, fantasy can help us to imagine things we might not otherwise be able to and may well inspire us to action. An example of the transformative power of fantasy film is seen in Tim Burton's 2010 adaptation of Lewis Carroll's novels *The Adventures of Alice in Wonderland* (1865) and *Through the Looking Glass, and What Alice Found There* (1871).

Alice's transformation in Wonderland

One definition of the verb 'to wonder' is to speculate about something, to consider 'what if?' Wonder can also be used as a noun to indicate something marvellous or the state of awed admiration that one feels in the presence of the wonderful, created world where 'anything can happen' (Warner 1995: xvi). The diegetic world of Burton's fantasy film elicits both meanings. For Alice, Wonderland is full of mysterious laws, practices and language, so that she feels generally unsure of herself and is forced to wonder, and to question everything. And clearly Wonderland is realized as a magical place where anything can happen and Alice is not bound by the laws of the everyday world. So Wonderland as it is represented in the film induces a state of wonder in the viewer, whether diegetic or extra-diegetic

Names are clearly important both to the original stories, and to Burton's re-imagined film version. It is likely that the audience comes to the film already in some way aware of Wonderland as an alternative, fantasy space. However we learn that the name of this magical realm is not 'Wonderland' but really 'Underland' (and that when Alice was there as a child she called it 'Wonderland' by mistake). Of course the change of name alerts us to a significant theme of the story, which is that we should never assume to know the nature of things because, rather than being fixed and secure, identity is unstable. The new name of Underland also invokes ideas of 'underworld', which carries the meanings of somewhere below the surface of the earth, the mythical region inhabited by the dead, and, paradoxically, can also be used to refer to the terrestrial world (i.e. the world we live in). The multiple meanings of both names (Wonderland/Underland) further suggest the polysemic nature of the story's alternative world, which generates many more puzzles to be solved than there are answers for them.

The film's action takes place after Alice's original childhood adventures in Wonderland which form the hazy back-story to events. In the second scene Alice, now aged 19, is attending a garden party that turns out to be arranged in celebration of her engagement to Lord Hamish, the son of one of her recently deceased father's business partners. Significantly this story begins where a traditional fairy tale ends, at the point where the heroine secures a husband. Hamish is a suitable match in many ways, but not in terms of satisfying Alice's wishes for how she would like her life to be. Hamish proposes publicly before the party guests and it seems that Alice has no choice but to accept. Her entrapment within the constraints of Victorian form and decorum expected of a young lady of her class is symbolized by the cage-like gazebo in which she and Hamish are standing. The claustrophobic atmosphere is further evoked by the quadrille that they dance prior to the proposal – in which couples perform a limited number of movements in close synchro-nization – and also by the limited colour palette (mostly variations of cream and pale blue with small amounts of yellow) used for the party guests' clothing. The restrictions of this highly mannered dance are contrasted with the freedom suggested by the flight of geese which Alice gazes up at from the confines of the dance floor, and with the riotous use of colours which subsequently greets her on arrival in Wonderland/Underland.

In the alternative fantasy space of Wonderland/Underland the laws of the everyday do not apply, and impossible things regularly occur – a body might suddenly shrink or grow big, a cat can appear out of nowhere and disappear again, animals speak so we may (or may not) understand. Whilst Wonderland/ Underland does not very much resemble how the world of the everyday looks and works, it is similar in the respect that Alice is expected to behave in certain ways. In the world Alice has come from it is presumed that she will accept Hamish's proposal of marriage because she is a girl of marriageable age at a time when the suitable career for girls of her class is to get married and bear children. And in Wonderland/Underland she is expected to slay the Red Queen's creature the Jabberwocky on the Frabjous Day (a seemingly impossible task), and to serve the Red Queen (a seemingly impossible person to please). Indeed Wonderland/Underland mirrors the everyday Victorian society in the way it automatically seeks to control Alice, and in turn this highlights fantasy's potential to make us look sideways at the everyday world and see things we otherwise would not be able to. Burton says that for him the film is 'a story about somebody using . . . this kind of world to figure out problems and things in their own life. . . . It's how we use those things to deal with our issues in life' (in Clark 2010). This statement clearly expresses one of the chief functions of fantasy besides entertainment, which is as a combination of teacher, life coach and prophet.

In Carroll's original stories Alice is a young child of 'seven and a half, exactly' (2010: 46), who falls asleep either out of doors (in *Wonderland*), or in a drawing room (in *Through the Looking Glass*), and dreams the fantasy events. So Wonderland and the real, waking world are distinct and separate from one another. In these stories Alice is only concerned with some small matters of everyday life such as her cat Dinah and her kittens. In Burton's film Alice is situated between Victorian childhood and adulthood, and is forced to confront one of life's threshold moments, marriage. This time it is not clear whether we are meant to understand that Alice's adventure in Wonderland/Underland really happens, or whether she is knocked unconscious from a fall and dreams her visit. Evidence to support the second premise includes elements that are mirrored in the everyday. For example, the twin sisters who tell Alice of Hamish's intention to propose are re-interpreted in Wonderland/Underland as twin brothers Tweedledum and Tweedledee. And Hamish's mother's anger at the white roses in the place of the red roses she asked for turns up in

Wonderland/Underland in the form of the Red Queen's exact same problem in her rose garden.

This doubling device is reminiscent of *The Wizard of Oz* in which we find key people in Dorothy's life in Kansas repeated in Oz. In both cases we can take this repetition as evidence that the magical worlds that Alice/Dorothy go to are real only in their dream/unconscious lives. We all carry the day's residue, especially things that trouble us in our waking life, into our dreams. It is widely acknowledged that one of the functions of dreams is as a problem-solving exercise and that 'most dreams are groping to understand problems that cannot yet be adequately grasped at' (French and Fromm cited in Levin 1990: 31). We can add another function of fantasy to our list then, in addition to those of teacher, life coach and prophet, and that is the job of exploration and articulation of difficult problems. For example, like Carroll's Alice, Burton's Alice suffers from a crisis of identity, being unsure of who she is and what she wants from life, and it is the fantasy part of the story that helps her to see and understand herself more clearly.

Alice's self-doubt at the start of the film is signalled by the physical changes (shrinking and growing) she experiences in Wonderland/Underland that happen suddenly and which she struggles to control. Her identity is repeatedly challenged when she first arrives there and there is considerable word play around whether she is the 'right Alice'. The first conversation between Alice and Absolem, the blue caterpillar, hinges on the idea of mistaken identity: he says 'Who are you?' Alice responds with a question ('Absolem?') which he takes to be an answer and replies 'You're not Absolem. I'm Absolem. The question is who are you?' When she replies 'Alice' his response is 'We shall see'. Alice then asks 'What do you mean by that? I ought to know who I am' and he replies 'Yes, you ought, stupid girl'. Absolem then temporarily settles the matter (and confuses it at the same time) by saying 'Is she the right Alice? Not hardly'. This rather odd exchange gets to Alice's central problem, which is that she is yet to really know who she is.

Throughout her visit Alice gradually comes to appreciate the ways of Wonderland/Underland, and as a result forms a sense of her own identity and capabilities. She learns how to harness the power of various foods to change her size when she needs to. More importantly she arrives at a sense of herself as someone able to solve problems, act on her own initiative, do battle and make her own life choices. The climactic scene where she slays the Jabberwocky whilst dressed in shining (heroic) medieval armour is the moment where this positive self-image is crystallized. In the books Alice is a child at the start of the stories and is still a child at the end. Though she goes through a great many adventures she does not demonstrate any life-changing transformation. Burton's film, however, follows the pattern discussed earlier as common to myths and tales identified by Eliade as 'initiation', which is also called 'coming of age' (1963: 201). In these stories the hero (and therefore the reader/ viewer's stand-in) goes through a series of trials, a journey (either to heaven or hell), and a marriage. Yet it is significant that in this film the prospect of marriage is one of the problems to be solved rather than a happy end.

Burton's film reflects on the importance of the imagination for problem solving and it is clear that imagination has a cognitive function. In order to ignite imagination the mind must be actively engaged rather than remain in a passive, receptive mode. As Alice begins to solve the various puzzles presented to her, and as she achieves the seemingly impossible tasks, she begins to see herself differently. She also realizes (in both senses of the word: (1) becomes aware of and also (2) performs) her own potential as a woman-warrior able to defeat the Jabberwocky. In doing so she completes another transformation into an adult. As we have discussed, 'coming of age' is one of the most common story types in fantasy, dealing with important threshold moments in life, and this film illustrates well how fantasy might contribute to the transformation of the individual. It is precisely the fantasy space of Wonderland/Underland that has precipitated the change in Alice by allowing her the opportunity to see herself and her place in the real world differently. This change is signalled on her return to the gazebo when she is able to refuse Hamish's proposal and negotiate an apprenticeship with his father (in her late father's business).

With this apprenticeship comes the freedom for Alice to be independent and self-sufficient, something only usually granted to men in Victorian society. Alice can now go out into the world and pursue her ideas of a new trade route to China. The final sequence of the film is of her on board a ship, significantly called 'Wonder', and she is looking out at the sea ahead. She has a blue

Figure 1.1 Alice and Absolem transformed in *Alice in Wonderland*

butterfly on her shoulder, who we assume to be a metamorphosed Absolem, a symbol of her own transformation (Figure 1.1). It is noteworthy that the ship is about to set sail, signalling the start of a new adventure, and that she stands at its prow, metaphorically in command of the vessel and by extension in control of her own destiny.

Alice is able to complete this transformation because of the new understanding of herself she gains in Wonderland/Underland. This understanding is enabled by the paradoxical ability of fantasy to make real or give the appearance of reality to something that otherwise exists only as potential, such as thought, or imagination. In the first scene of the film Alice's father says that 'believing in the impossible is the only way to make it possible', meaning that once a thought is rendered into words or images we may be able to perceive that it can happen. A useful term taken from Rosemary Jackson (1998: 19) to help us express this transformative power of fantasy is 'alterity'. Alterity is the state of being different or 'other'. It also carries the sense of exchanging one's perspective for that of the 'other', perhaps by means of a mirror image, and therefore also suggests distortion, alteration and change. For Alice Wonderland/Underland plays a crucial role of fantasy and allows her to experience alterity, to see herself and her world differently. Certainly fantasy films of all kinds may provide us with a similar function; they can help us to wonder 'what if' because they realize images in which we too might glimpse alterity.

The world that we discover in fantasy is often, like the one Alice experienced, very like our own but also unlike ours in important ways. And it is not only at threshold moments of our lives that we benefit from experiencing fantasy, but also throughout the whole of life. This is because when we are immersed in the story world we are separated from our real world and this can enable us to negotiate emotional problems, anxieties and fears in the safe protected space of story play. Child psychologist Bruno Bettelheim (1991 [1976]) clearly articulates the value of fantasy stories such as the fairy tale in a child's development into an emotionally healthy adult. Since his death in 1990 Bettelheim has been widely criticized for his various failings as a theoretician and practitioner (for example Zipes 2002: 179–205), whilst at the same time being praised for acknowledging the role that stories play in the socialization process.

The essence of Bettelheim's argument is the commonsense notion that fairy tales are good for children. The kind of stories offered by fantasy, especially fairy tales and heroic myths, specifically address our fundamental need 'to find meaning in our lives' (Bettelheim 1991: 3). Second to the child's need for support from parental figures is a need to feel part of a group, and fairy tales, according to Bettelheim, transmit cultural heritage in the right manner to provide a sense of belonging. For him, stories should entertain, arouse curiosity, stimulate the imagination, help to develop the intellect and clarify emotions (Bettelheim 1991: 5). Whereas myths involve the heroic deeds of gods and superhuman mortals, the heroes of fairy tales are usually ordinary people, often children (with whom the young reader may readily identify). The simple structure of the fairy tale, its dreamlike feel which amplifies experiences, and formulaic style, helps the child to safely confront fears and anxieties that would otherwise be hard for them to engage with. The argument goes that as their in-story surrogates are seen to achieve victory despite overwhelming odds, this helps to enable the (child) audience to understand themselves, their own emotional processes, to overcome self-doubt and to arrive at an empowered feeling of maturity and self-worth (Bettelheim 1991).

We may see this process at work in Burton's *Alice in Wonderland*, as Alice is transformed by her experience in the fantasy space of Wonderland/Underland and returns to her everyday world with fresh insight into who she is, what she is capable of and what she wants from her life.

In addition to these feelings of self-confident agency, the child achieves an understanding of their own unconscious feelings, Bettelheim says, 'by spinning out daydreams – ruminating, rearranging, and fantasizing about suitable story elements in response to unconscious pressures' (1991: 7). For Bettelheim, the symbolic elements of fairy tales 'offer new dimensions to the child's imagination which would be impossible' for the child to discover alone (1991: 7). Furthermore, he says that 'the form and structure of fairy tales suggest images to the child by which [they] can structure [their] daydreams and with them give better direction to [their] life' (Bettelheim 1991: 7). It is only by giving form to fears and anxieties that we are able to work them through and come to terms with them. Bettelheim (1991) says that certain kinds of fantasy help us to do this: fairy tales for children and heroic fantasy for adults. Fantasy film might perform a similar therapeutic function, as unconscious dramas may be played out, aided by the identificatory process where the viewer can place themselves at the centre of the narrative. As the viewer becomes part of the action they are able to experience what it would be like to be someone else. This possibility of vicarious transcendent identification is explored in James Cameron's 2009 fantasy science fiction film *Avatar*.

Avatar *and identification*

In *Avatar* an ex-US marine, Jake Sully, merges his human identity with the body of an alien humanoid (Na'vi) on the moon Pandora. A definition of an avatar is a digital representation which acts in a virtual world, an online, or on-screen alter ego. The idea of an avatar can be used to think about the spectator's experience of cinema, where we routinely identify with on-screen characters. The idea of an avatar can also be used to think about the experience of fantasy, where we may fantasize about living out a specific scenario, and/or about being someone else. And the avatar in *Avatar* further reflects on the value of escape into fantasy and the importance of storytelling.

Jake lives out the concept of the avatar as stand-in on a number of levels. On one level he stands in for his dead twin brother who was originally trained to 'drive' the avatar. On another level we see similar connections operating in the relationship between the Na'vi and their animals. The Na'vi enjoy a magical, spiritual link to the animals they ride and fly on, plugging their neural queues (ponytails) into their mounts' antennae to create the *shahaylu*, the bond through which they experience one another and communicate. When Jake's avatar is joined to his direhorse (a Pandoran horse) or banshee (Figure 1.2) via the neural interface there is a relay of links. Jake is connected to his avatar and the avatar is connected to his mount, while the cinema spectator is connected, via a similar *shahaylu*-type identification with the on-screen events, to all three.

These connections literalize Christian Metz's notion of 'secondary cinematic identification in the cinema' in which the spectator identifies with diegetic characters (1982: 56). There is also a strong sense of Metz's primary identification, which is with the act of looking itself, and with the camera, giving the spectator the illusion of agency and a feeling of power because the camera is able to go anywhere and see anything (1982: 97). Jake thus represents the viewer who, in the act of identification with their on-screen

Figure 1.2 The *shahaylu* bond between Jake and his banshee in *Avatar*

surrogate, is directly linked to the diegetic action and assumes a connection through affinity and recognition. His connection resembles the spectator–screen identificatory model in that his avatar allows him to live out a fantasy of an enriched existence just as the film viewer can live out an enriched existence when identifying with the on-screen character who is commonly superior in some way (more handsome, braver, more intelligent, fitter, more skilled, more athletic, and their lives more exciting, romantic, fortunate or dangerous).

The idea of an enriched diegetic existence is doubly poignant in *Avatar* as in the real world Jake has lost the use of his legs. When connected to his avatar he can enjoy full use of his limbs, and better yet, his avatar is ten feet tall, lithe, fit, and extremely athletic. For Jake, his dreaming projected self is able to vicariously live out his fantasy of mobility; his avatar can walk and run and also fly. (The human urge for freedom is commonly expressed in the desire for flight and linked to the phenomenon of the lucid dream in which the empowered dreamer is able to manipulate the dream-action.) Jake's avatar does all this in a truly mythic, fantasy landscape where he is accepted into the indigenous Na'vi society.

Many traditional or archaic groups (like those represented by the Na'vi, who place great emphasis on the role of oral story in the maintenance of their cultural traditions) centre their storytelling on a shamanic figure. The shaman has privileged access to special knowledge and is prized for their ability, among other things, to weave special knowledge into tales to educate, entertain and guide their audience. The shaman (similar to the dreamwalker of some cultures) journeys by means of a trance 'during which his [sic] soul is believed to leave his [sic] body and ascend to the sky or descend to the underworld' (Eliade 1974: 5). The shaman, like Neytiri's Mother Moat, and like Jake (and therefore by extension the viewer), is able through dedicated training, natural talent, and special privilege, to travel to a fantastical place, a spirit world, where they have experiences not open to the ordinary person. They go in order to find answers, or to speak to and influence the inhabitants of that world. They then bring back messages and wisdom from, or impressions of, the other world in order to benefit the society from which they travelled. There is a social gain from the shamanic journey, but there is also a personal gain for the traveller who gets to escape to another world and witness special events. Jake's avatar can be seen as a dreamwalker because he journeys between the world of the Na'vi and the human base where he is expected to record his experiences on the video log and share intelligence (either scientific or military). To the film viewer both Jake and his avatar are dreamwalkers which the viewer, through the process of identification, sends into the other fantasy story world, and they exist to bring back stories to the audience.

As well as being a self-reflexive film about film as storyteller, and about how the spectator might be interpolated into the diegetic action, *Avatar*'s themes also explore American history in terms of the wars between the colonizers and the Native American nations over land, presenting the American corporation as single-minded and brutal in their quest for the prophetically named 'unobtanium'. The film presents Na'vi culture in nostalgic terms as a utopian image of social and ecological harmony in contrast to the morally bankrupt American 'aliens'. We are taken on an exciting outward journey to the fabulous story world, and also offered a journey inwards, where we might gain insights about ourselves and our own world. Because analogy and metaphor are so readily applied to fantasy as in this example, it can be used as a dream factory, a magical mirror, or a land of the spirits, wherein we may glimpse enlightenment and return to our own world transformed and refreshed.

It is exactly this transformation of vision that Tolkien saw as the particular 'gift' of fantasy, which he named 'recovery'. He believed in the power of fantasy, in the imaginative creation of images of things (such as a secondary story world) not actually present, to alter the way we look at our everyday (primary) world, so that we (re-)gain a clear view (Tolkien 1966: 77). For example, one of the conflicts played out in *Avatar* is between the corporation who want the unobtanium because it will bring them material wealth, and the Na'vi who live on the land in which the mineral is found. The story is narrated in such a way that the viewer is aligned with the Na'vi against their aggressors, and the ecological destruction done to Na'vi territory is seen unequivocally as an evil act. Therefore we might draw analogies between the diegetic action and events in our everyday world and see them differently as a result. In this way a fantasy film like *Avatar* not only reflects but also arguably has the potential to influence social discourse, so that a change in opinions and ideologies may feed back into the social world. A function of Tolkien's 'recovery' is that we are able to achieve a fresh perspective as a result of our journey to the secondary world and be able to see '"things as we are (or were) meant to see them"' and thus gain a renewed view of reality (1966: 77).

After 'recovery', Tolkien's second great gift of fantasy – and we all know that in the land of story there are usually three gifts, or three wishes, or three trials – is 'escape'. Tolkien sees escape as one of the main functions of the fairy story, but the term does not, for him, carry the negative connotations (for which he blames critics) that we questioned earlier. Instead he means the word to be understood as 'departure' and 'imagination'. Escape, Tolkien says, 'is evidently as a rule very practical, and may even be heroic' (1966: 79). It enables us to gain insight, and to learn again the value of things which we might else have forgotten (Tolkien 1966: 79–85).

Tolkien's third and final term to describe the gift bestowed upon us by fantasy is 'consolation'. This is the joy we feel at the miraculous or surprising turn of the happy ending from the possibility of tragedy. Tolkien calls this moment *eucatastrophe*, when catastrophe is averted: 'the *eucatastrophic* tale is the true form of fairy-tale and its highest function' (1966: 85, emphasis in original). In *Avatar* the consolatory *eucatastrophic* moment occurs after the Na'vi have won their war and have sent the 'aliens' home; Neytiri has carried Jake's human body to the Tree of Souls and she lays it alongside his avatar. At this point we know that Ewya is attempting to transfer Jake's consciousness permanently to his avatar and there is a pause while we wait to see if he will die (like Dr Augustine) or miraculously be reborn. Suddenly his avatar eyes snap open and gaze into the camera lens. The film ends.

This ending resolves a second conflict in the film between characteristics of the science fiction genre and those of the fantasy genre, battle-lines which are also drawn along the division between the corporation and the indigenous people. In the end fantasy triumphs, not only because the Na'vi have won, but also because at the moment of his resurrection to his new life, Jake and his avatar are now one being and he no longer has to leave the fantasy world to return to the real world as the fantasy has become his reality.

This is not so for the cinema viewer though, who must exit the fantasy, despite having the consolation of the happy ending. This might lead us to the conclusion that the viewer is left with a fresh sense of loss brought about by the comparison of the (utopian) fantasy film world, where wishes are often temporarily fulfilled, and the world outside, where wishes are newly unsatisfied. Whether or not we re-emerge into our everyday world better off for having made the journey into fantasy, we suggest that there is a satisfaction in the idea that there remains a place of refuge and escape (with its attendant gifts of recovery and consolation) to which we may return, at will, where everyday rules do not necessarily apply. And this place is not just in our imagination or dreams, but a place that we can access through fantasy's magic portal: the rabbit-hole, the looking glass, the wardrobe, the avatar, the cinema screen.

FANTASY AND FILM GENRE

In previous sections we have established the heritage of traditional storytelling drawn on by fantasy film, and also thought about some of the purposes to which fantasy may be put. This preparatory work to identify the nature of the source material of fantasy film, and some of its potential value for the social and individual lives of audiences, has hopefully equipped us to more easily recognize a fantasy text when we see it and to understand where the limits and borders between fantasy and its relatives might lie. We now move on to think about the difficulties of genre classification in general, and to consider ways in which film fantasy may usefully be defined.

The concept of genre has been a significant factor in the development of film theory because of its associations with Hollywood, and because of the implications for cinema as an economic, commodity-producing system and medium of mass entertainment (see Neale 2000; Langford 2005). Genre is also important because it links the film industry to the film audience, and because understanding genre helps audiences, critics and scholars to understand films both as parts of systems that have developed through time, and as existing at any particular moment. There are a number of issues to reflect on when we attempt to understand the fantasy film genre, and the first task is to try to overcome the problem of how to understand the term 'fantasy' itself.

This is seemingly a harder task than it would first appear. Discussions of film genre rarely linger very long on the subject of fantasy except to remark that the borders between the three cinefantastic genres of horror, science fiction and fantasy tend to blur. Often this is all the mention that fantasy gets before the discussion moves on to the other two genres leaving fantasy to languish somewhere in the margins. But why is this? In her recent study of fantasy film Katherine Fowkes remarks that 'if conceptualizing fantasy as a genre proves elusive and messy at times, it may say as much about the concept of genre as it does about fantasy' (2010: 3). Certainly the subject of genre is about as sprawling and contentious as the subject of fantasy. Indeed, one of the reasons that fantasy film is under discussed is that the term 'fantasy' is used to cover a wide variety of forms that seem difficult to manage in any single genre. Clute and Grant indicate the scale of this difficulty. They say that the term can be used to refer to all sorts of stories: 'involving dreams and visions, allegory and romance, surrealism and magic realism, satire, and wonderland, supernatural fiction, dark fantasy, weird fiction and horror . . . sometimes expressing conflicting understandings of the nature of fantasy' (Clute and Grant 1997: viii).

Therefore the vast scope of fantasy is the first obstacle to any attempt at categorization. Jackson acknowledges this difficulty when she notes that the word 'fantastic' has its roots in a Greek term 'meaning to make visible or manifest' (1998: 13). 'In this general sense', she says, 'all imaginary activity is fantastic, all literary works are fantasies' (Jackson 1998: 13). If all literary works are fantasies, then it follows that all films to some extent are fantasies too. The term fantasy would certainly in some ways seem to apply to all narrative fiction films, which strive to 'produce illusions based on the manipulation of an original pro-filmic event by various forms of photographic and montage effect' (Sobchack 1996: 312). As a result we could potentially label any film a fantasy because it is in some way a fiction.

However as a medium based on photography, which is concerned with capturing the verisimilitude of an object or event placed before the camera, film might appear to naturally favour realism. But as a medium which has mostly been concerned with telling stories, and bearing in mind the element of innate fantasy in all forms of artistic representation, it should also be recognized that film harnesses and exploits its aura of verisimilitude in the service of fiction and, by extension, fantasy. This leaves us with a dilemma and invites us to question fantasy film's relationship to 'reality'. Kathryn Hume (1984) provides a way to reconcile and accommodate these two opposing ideas of film as a realist art and film as concerned with the creation of fictions.

In her study of fantasy and mimesis Hume seeks the broadest possible description of fantasy and settles on the term 'fantasy impulse' which she sets alongside the 'mimetic impulse', declaring them equally important to narrative (1984: 25). All literature, Hume says, is the product of these two impulses, to varying degrees. Mimesis is 'felt as the desire to imitate, to describe events, people, situations, and objects with such verisimilitude that others can share your experience; and fantasy [is] the desire to change givens and alter reality' (Hume 1984: 20). Fantasy then is '*any departure from consensus reality*, an impulse' (Hume 1984: 21, emphasis in original). For Hume this fantasy impulse (which is also taken up by David Butler in *Fantasy Cinema: Impossible Worlds on Screen*, 2009) leads to the creation of story worlds that include any scenario that departs from what is possible according to the laws of our world, including immortality, alternate worlds and universes, marvels considered real, miracles and monsters (1984: 21). Brian Attebery refers to Hume's work, adding that whilst mimesis and fantasy are contrasting (he refers to them as 'modes') they are not opposites and they usually:

> coexist within any given work; there are no purely mimetic or fantastic works of fiction. Mimesis without fantasy would be nothing but reporting one's perceptions of actual events. Fantasy without mimesis would be a purely artificial invention, without recognizable objects or actions.
>
> (1992: 3)

But this is not to say that the terms fantasy and mimesis have no value for us. Indeed, they are very important. In particular they are essential to an understanding of the core debates about realism and fantasy that we return to in Chapter 2.

In the meantime we can consider Attebery's suggestion of three ways to organize fantasy, each of which requires a shift in scale and focus (1992: 1–17). The widest focus is accounted for by the term 'mode'; the narrowest 'formula', and between these two extremes sits 'genre'. The term 'mode' is useful because as a close relation to Hume's 'impulse' it involves the idea of fantasy as an approach and an attitude. The fantasy mode is much larger than, and encompasses, the fantasy genre. Jackson also writes about the literary fantastic as a mode, using the following quote from Fredric Jameson for clarification:

> For when we speak of a mode, what can we mean but that this particular type of literary discourse is not bound to the conventions of a given age, nor indissolubly linked to a given type of verbal artefact, but rather persists as a temptation and a mode of expression across a whole range of historical periods, seeming to offer itself, if only intermittently, as a formal possibility which can be revived and renewed.
>
> (Jameson 1975 quoted in Jackson 1998: 7)

Jameson's words help to explain that a mode occupies a much larger territory than a genre. Looked at this way, as a mode, fantasy is not restricted to any particular form, and accommodates the whole range of story and pre-story forms we discussed earlier, such as cave paintings, plays, oral folktales, literary fairy tales and film. In fact the fantasy mode may be found in any artefact (image, text, articulation) that deals with matters of the imagination, with fancy, with the impossible, and that which makes the hidden or invisible visible.

So as a mode fantasy exists conceptually across time and space. Fantasy is a way of thinking. Fantasy is also a way of expressing, and it is a language. Fantasy as a mode maintains an attitude towards reality, takes liberties with rationality, is generous with and transgresses limits and boundaries and allows for the eruption of imagination-based events, into external reality. It is ahistorical because it exists throughout history, and global because it also exists across cultures. Mode is a term that accounts for a very broad range. Attebery describes the fantastic mode as 'a vast subject, taking in all literary manifestations of the imagination's ability to soar above the merely possible' (1992: 2). Although Attebery refers to literature, mode is not medium-specific and applies equally well to film.

At the other end of the descriptive scale from mode is 'formula', often used as a derogatory term in conjunction with fantasy, whether in literature, game or film form, to refer to a 'commercial product, with particular authors or publishers' lines serving as brand names for the consumer' (Attebery 1992: 2). Formula is perceived by Attebery as 'restrictive in scope, recent in origin, and specialized in audience and appeal', and its 'success depends on consistency and predictability' (1992: 2). His summary of formulaic fantasy involves a story that combines stock characters and devices with a predictable plot in which good ultimately triumphs over evil. Certain film cycles can become associated with formulaic fantasy, particularly where there are sequels or 'look alikes' that quickly follow on from the success of earlier films, examples being the cluster of sword and sorcery films that emerged in the 1980s: Hawk the Slayer (1980), The Beastmaster (1982), Conan the Barbarian (1982), The Sword and the Sorcerer (1982), Krull (1983), Conan the Destroyer (1984) and Red Sonja (1985). Therefore, if mode is wide, ahistorical and flexible, then formula is extremely narrow, prescriptive and fixed in form, though not to any particular time or place.

Genre is narrower than mode yet broader than formula. Like mode, genres are varied, elastic, and receptive to artistic development but call on a boundaried set of conventions and iconography. Whereas mode is ahistorical, genres, as Steve Neale notes, 'are always historically relative, and therefore historically specific' (1995: 464). This means that genres and subgenres are dynamic and fluctuate in use and popularity. Generic change occurs in response to social, cultural or political influence as well as economic determinants, and a genre's conventions change as they 'embody the crucial ideological concerns' of their time (Fiske 1987: 110). Moreover, Neale asserts that genres may also help to shape audience values (1980: 16), whilst in Tools for Cultural Studies Tony Thwaites, Lloyd Davis and Warwick Mules describe the relationship as reciprocal: 'a genre develops according to social conditions; transformations in genre and texts can influence and reinforce social conditions' (1994: 100). Occasionally subgenres might become dormant for a period and then re-emerge, perhaps in response to social change or in order to take advantage of innovations in technology.

It should be evident by this point that, as Barry Keith Grant summarizes, 'genre movies are those commercial feature films which, through repetition and variation, tell familiar stories with familiar characters in familiar situations' (1986: ix). In *An Introduction to Film Studies* Paul Watson breaks this down further:

> each genre is a rule-governed territory, one which shares a conven-
> tionality not only of visual imagery, but more complexly of particular
> expectations of plot and narrative structure, and how these, in turn,
> motivate and justify the specificities of props, costume, milieus and
> subject matter within and across the generic spectrum.

> (2003: 157)

How, then, do we make sense of all this? What are the conventions shared by fantasy film? What characteristics should we expect to see in the fantasy genre and subgenres? And what kinds of films might be excluded from the genre?

Vivian Sobchack (1996) is one of the few critics to provide a working definition of fantasy film, though she does group together fantasy adventure with horror and science fiction under the overall heading of 'The Fantastic'. This close association between fantasy, horror and science fiction is commonly referred to, drawing attention to the tendency of genre, as Watson writes, to routinely emerge as a 'border dispute: defining the boundaries between one genre and another' (2003: 154). The reason why the divisions between these three genres blur is because, as Sobchack notes, each of them 'imaginatively constructs alternative – "fantastic" – worlds and tells stories of impossible experiences that defy rational logic and currently known empirical laws' (1996: 312). Quoting Tom Hutchinson, Sobchack says that horror 'is the appalling ideas given sudden flesh; science fiction is the improbable made possible within the confines of a technological age' (1974 in Sobchack 1996: 312). She adds that 'fantasy adventure and romance is the appealing and impossible personal wish concretely and objectively fulfilled' (Sobchack 1996: 312).

In separating out fantasy from its near neighbours of horror and science fiction Sobchack considers those films that she excludes from her working definition of fantasy film. For example, according to her a number of film forms 'in which non-naturalistic elements are predominant' should be kept out of the fantasy genre (Sobchack 1996: 312). These are: avant-garde, animation, musicals and biblical epics. Avant-garde and experimental films are excluded by Sobchack unless they specifically and overtly reference non-film fantasy forms such as the fairy tale, because they are not part of the institutional model of commercial studio production and popular media, being more likely to be 'high' culture (1996: 313). She also notes that the biblical epic is excluded because bible stories are usually understood as historically accurate and/or allegorical rather than fantasy (Sobchack 1996: 313). The animated film is left out 'unless, like *Gulliver's Travels* (1939), it also draws upon material previously associated with those genres' (Sobchack 1996: 313). This is because Sobchack's definition of fantasy is related to Tzvetan Todorov's notion of the fantastic, where the viewer/reader must move from realism into fantasy, and 'without this realist underpinning, the "fantastic" aspects of the created world and the "special" effects which bring them to visibility would have no normative ground upon which their fantastic qualities and their specialness could be figured' (1996: 313).

The action in *The Wizard of Oz*, for example, qualifies as having 'realist underpinning' as it moves from the everyday world of Kansas into the world of Oz, and there are two ways to think about where this realm might actually be, and these readings can be used to illustrate Todorov's (1975) explanation of the fantastic. One reading of events in *The Wizard of Oz* is that Dorothy is magically transported to Oz following her wish to find somewhere 'over the rainbow' where 'there isn't any trouble'. According to this view Oz is a real (secondary world) place, and the events that occur are real and logically consistent within the terms of this magical land. Conversely, it could be argued that all of the events that occur in Oz take place in Dorothy's mind as she lies unconscious after receiving a bump on the head when the twister strikes her aunt and uncle's farm, and the viewer is merely given a privileged insight into her intersubjective dream.

This hesitation that the viewer feels, between two separate readings, is key to Todorov's definition of the fantastic. Whereas the term 'the fantastic' has in some ways become synonymous with fantasy film in general, Todorov's explanation of fantastic literature is extremely narrow and very particular and states that the fantastic genre 'occupies the duration of . . . uncertainty' about the nature of what is being experienced (1975: 25). He writes, 'In a world which is indeed our world, the one we know, a world without devils, sylphides, or vampires, there occurs an event which cannot be explained by the laws of this same familiar world' (Todorov 1975: 25). Todorov says that we must then decide whether we are a 'victim of an illusion of the senses, of a product of the imagination' in which case there has been no violation of the natural laws, or whether the event is real and therefore the world 'is controlled by laws unknown to us' (1975: 25). The fantastic is located in the moment of indecision and hesitancy between these two explanations. If the matter is settled as being an illusory, imagined event, then the story belongs to the subcategory of the uncanny, and if the event is real and takes place in a real (albeit secondary, fantasy) world, then the story belongs to the subcategory of the marvellous. In The Wizard of Oz we can choose to either believe in the marvellous (Oz is a real place) or in realism (Oz is a dream). But whilst we hesitate between these two readings and remain undecided about which to privilege, we are in the realm of the fantastic.

Before Dorothy's journey to Oz, by whatever means, imagination or magic, we are on familiar ground, in a world we in general recognize as our own. This initial grounding in realism is an essential quality of fantasy for Sobchack. She says that the 'fantasy film proper starts from an initial realism which is then violated when the monster emerges or the dead come to life' (Sobchack 1996: 313). Todorov's definition of the fantastic also starts in the world we know as it must in order to sustain any doubt about the nature of the story's status (i.e. uncanny, fantastic or marvellous). This helps to delineate Todorov and Sobchack's understanding of the very specific term 'the fantastic'. It also makes apparent that we need other ways of considering those fantasy stories which do not conform to this particular definition, such as those whose events take place entirely in a secondary world like The Lord of the Rings. A different system is needed that makes allowance for a wide range of story, setting and character types, is narrower in scope than 'mode' and wider in scope than 'the fantastic' (and formula), and also allows for the boundary disputes between fantasy, horror and science fiction to be acknowledged.

Louis Giannetti offers one potential solution to this need in *Understanding Movies* (2005) where he uses the idea of a continuum to express the separation and overlap between realism and formalism. This continuum has significance for fantasy films because, like most fiction films, they fall somewhere between these two extremes. 'Formalist' (also known as expressionist) refers to a type of 'stylistically flamboyant' film that has a 'high degree of manipulation', and a 'stylization of reality' which is often highly subjective (Giannetti 2005: 4). Giannetti says that:

> Formalists are not much concerned with how realistic their images are, but with their beauty or power. The most artificial genres – musicals, sci-fi, fantasy film – are generally classified as formalist . . . [Whereas realism's] filmmakers are more concerned with what's being shown rather than how it's manipulated.
>
> (2005: 4–8)

Therefore Giannetti places avant-garde formalism at one end of his continuum, and documentary realism at the other. He then suggests that classical cinema belongs between these two extremes as it is an 'intermediate style that avoids the extremes of realism and formalism – though most movies in the classical form lean toward one or the other style' (Giannetti 2005: 4).

In his critical survey of fantasy film Alec Worley (2005) takes Giannetti's continuum model and applies it to the fantastic genres science fiction, fantasy and horror in order to express the relationships between them. He describes science fiction at one end of a line and fantasy at the other, and considers where some genre films might fit in (Figure 1.3). Plausible realist science-based films such as *2001: A Space Odyssey* (1968) could be put at the end of the science fiction section, and more 'eccentric' science fiction with little real emphasis on technology or science, such as *Bill and Ted's Excellent Adventure* (1988), may be positioned towards the implausible fantasy sections (Worley 2005: 11). *Star Wars* would occupy a place at the fantasy end of science fiction, perhaps at a place marked science fantasy (Worley 2005: 11).

Horror films might also fit on this kind of hypothetical scale with rational realist horror such as *Seven* (1995) towards one end, and dark fantasy (*El laberinto del fauno/Pan's Labyrinth*, 2006) towards the other, formalist end (Figure 1.4). Supernatural fantasy horror, such as *What Lies Beneath* (2000) or *Sleepy Hollow* (1999), would be placed between the two ends. Worley's distinction between fantasy and horror is that fantasy is usually associated with 'some form of healing', allied to the transformation function, or Tolkien's 'consolation', and whereas the horror film's 'ultimate concern . . . is death – whether it comes dressed as a werewolf, a vampire or a chainsaw-lugging lunatic . . . fantasy clings to life' (2005: 12).

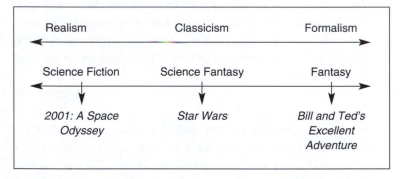

Figure 1.3 Fantasy–science fiction continuum (adapted from Worley 2005: 11)

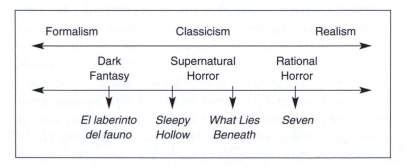

Figure 1.4 Fantasy–horror continuum (adapted from Worley 2005: 12)

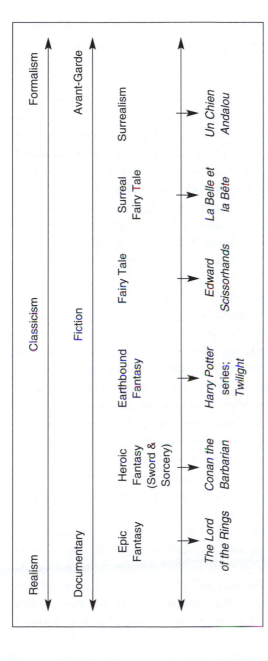

Figure 1.5 Fantasy continuum (adapted from Giannetti 2005: 4, and Worley 2005: 14)

For fantasy film Worley goes on to propose 'five separate subgenres of story, five loose sets of narrative scheme' (2005: 13–14). These subgenres are epic fantasy, heroic fantasy, earthbound fantasy, fairy tale and surrealism, and they also fall along the realism–formalism continuum. Figure 1.5 brings together and adapts Giannetti's scheme and Worley's model. As the name implies, earthbound fantasy includes films whose stories unfold in a world that we recognize as our own and involve the viewer identifying with characters who are like them, so it sits on the continuum, 'where magic and logic intersect', midway between the 'absurdist realism of fairy tale and the realistic absurdity of heroic fantasy' (Worley 2005: 83). The familiar everyday setting is the backdrop for some magic to unfold, so the adventures of Harry Potter fit into this category. In the earthbound story, magic either intrudes into the ordinary world, as in The Twilight Saga (2008–ongoing), or the hero, travelling through the ordinary world, finds him/herself in a magical place, like Narnia in The Chronicles of Narnia (currently 2005–2010).

At the expressionist end of Worley's scale lies surrealism, such as Luis Buñuel's Un Chien Andalou/An Andalusian Dog (1928). Between surrealism and earthbound fantasy lies fairy tale, a term that Worley uses loosely 'to include any kind of fable, folktale or fantasy allegory', which 'may employ all manner of weird phenomena without having to explain themselves, like . . . the worlds of the Disney fable' (2005: 14). Set between earthbound fantasy and realism lies the category of film that portrays a convincing representation of the fantasy it depicts (Worley 2005: 14). This is heroic fantasy which features characters such as Hercules, Conan or Achilles who are practically invincible. The world they inhabit is not usually our primary, ordinary world (though they can sometimes be found there), but a secondary story world, and they are concerned with magic and mysticism rather than the rational 'magic' of science, the province of science fiction.

Closest to the realism end of the fantasy continuum lies epic fantasy. The hero of the epic fantasy is a fallible 'courageous everyman striving to save an entire world and its people, prepared to sacrifice his own life in order to do so' (Worley 2005: 163). These heroes have a strong link to the world they inhabit, like Frodo does to The Shire and Middle Earth. Worley comments on the importance of myth to epic fantasy. He says that though myth's influence is felt throughout the fantasy genre, 'the full weight of myth itself rests on the shoulders of epic fantasy' (Worley 2005: 232). So the roots of this subgenre are in mythological story cycles such as Homer's *Iliad* and *Odyssey*, and the *Epic of Gilgamesh*, and as if to mark their ancestry epic fantasy films 'almost invariably take place in archaic worlds' (Worley 2005: 233).

Though these ideas of using continuums might raise questions about how best to label and describe fantasy, they demonstrate the useful process of identifying films that may be representative of certain kinds of fantasy subgenres. Attebery comments on this practice of definition based on 'descriptions after the fact; that is the critic assembles a body of texts that seem somehow to fit the term and then describes the common feature or features' (1992: 12). He compares this process to identifying 'territories on a map, with definitional limits' separating one category from another (Attebery 1992: 12). And this mapping out is one way of describing the method employed in constructing the continuums above. The continuum model also points to another method of categorization discussed by Attebery, which is to approach genres as 'fuzzy sets', therefore to define categories 'not by boundaries but by a center' (1992: 12). At the center of a fuzzy set are 'significant examples of what best represents it' (Clute and Grant 1997: viii). We might then allocate each of Worley's subgenres a fuzzy set and place the designated example at the centre. Clustered around the central definitive example will be films that share many characteristics with it, and those positioned farther away will share fewer characteristics with the central film, while still sharing features with their near neighbours.

Taking up Attebery's notion of fuzzy sets, Clute and Grant say that their own fantasy fuzzy sets are formed around this rough definition:

> a fantasy text is a self-coherent narrative which, when set in our reality, tells a story which is impossible in the world as we perceive it; when set in an otherworld or secondary world, that otherworld will be impossible, but stories set there will be possible *in the otherworld's terms.*
>
> (1997: viii, emphasis in original)

They identify a number of 'exemplary writers and motifs' that make up their 'significant examples' (centres of their fuzzy sets), but state that 'the boundaries of fantasy fade into water margins in every direction' and the water margins accommodate stories that do 'not initially look like fantasy' (Clute and Grant 1997: viii, emphasis in original). Clute defines water margins as 'the unmapped and ultimately unmappable regions which surround a central empire'; these regions make room for stories 'which marginally escape easy definition as fantasy' (1997: 997). It is possible to imagine those films that do not fit comfortably within the confines of the fantasy film fuzzy set occupying the water margins outlying the central regions; films such as *Das Cabinet des Dr Caligari/The Cabinet of Dr Caligari* (1920) in the fantasy–horror, and *Bill and Ted's Excellent Adventure* in the fantasy–science fiction water margins.

Our own voyage in this chapter is almost at an end. We have dipped our toes into story oceans, exposed the tangled roots and some of the uses of fantasy, traversed continuums, swum in unmapped waters and sighted fantasy fuzzy sets. It would seem that to set limits for the fantasy film is a Herculean task of epic proportions. We might conclude that it is against the very nature of fantasy to accept limits; fantasy adapts, it can cross boundaries and borders in ways that often resist categorization. Yet perhaps there are some common elements, themes, iconography or ideas we have encountered that may aid our approach to fantasy, and the heroic quests of others. We submit these along with a few indicative examples where appropriate to take on the journey towards further discovery.

At the heart of fantasy is magic (the *Harry Potter* series). Fantasy film imagines and realizes the magical and its synonyms: the impossible, the marvellous, the wondrous and the miraculous. This might be expressed as a magical place (*The Wizard of Oz*) or time (*Excalibur*, 1981), in magical events (*Clash of the Titans*, 1981), through magical characters (*Labyrinth*, 1986), or through magical transformation or metamorphosis (*La Belle et la Bête*, 1946). Fantasy film typically draws its subjects, themes, characters, events and settings from traditional story forms such as myth (*Jason and the Argonauts*, 1963), legend (*Robin Hood: Prince of Thieves*, 1991) and fairy tale (*The Company of Wolves*, 1984). Fantasy films may deal with the activities of magical characters, both of mythological origin (gods, demigods, angels, demons, superheroes, personifications of natural phenomena such as death and winter, and threshold guardians), legendary origin (pirates, highwaymen, knights errant, adventurers, and explorers) and of fairy tale origin (spirits, elves, sprites, fairies, goblins, shape-shifters, dwarves, fairy godmothers, frog princes, tin men, scarecrows, witches, necromancers, wizards, sorcerers, hobbits).

As fantasy circulates around the desires of ordinary people we also find mundane characters at the centre of many fantasy stories, often placed in extraordinary situations (servants, men, women, children, heroes), as well as people who represent nobility (kings, queens, princesses, princes, knights, barons). And the fantasy place might be inhabited by a number of fantasy creatures (unicorns, dragons, flying horses, Cyclops, enchanted beasts, talking animals, minotaurs, trolls, and giants), or mundane creatures (wolves, bears, horses, rats, mice, cats). Fantasy exploits may follow the figure of the hero on quests, both internal (*Alice in Wonderland*) and external (*Stardust*, 2007). They are concerned with struggles between good and evil (*Star Wars*), light and dark (*Legend*, 1985), law and lawlessness (*The Dark Knight*, 2008).

Fantasy films can be set entirely in a secondary story world such as Middle Earth, may move from a world we recognize into a magical secondary world such as Narnia, or may take place partly or entirely in a dreamscape. Fantasy might also concern itself with our own primary world into which has strayed some magical creature from another realm (*E.T.: The Extra-Terrestrial*, 1982), or some supernatural creature from the dreams of human beings such as angels (*Here Comes Mr Jordan*, 1941), and ghosts (*Ghost*, 1990). Sometimes we find stories about those who tumble into the magical realm by accident (*The Lion, the Witch and the Wardrobe*, 2005). Fantasy film is equally as adventurous in its temporal settings which extend over the whole of primordial and human history (*10,000 B.C.*, 2008), and include our mythical past (*Clash of the Titans*), medieval kingdoms (*Dragonslayer*, 1981) and feudal, chivalric or pastoral societies (*First Knight*, 1995), as well as modern-day cities (*Enchanted*, 2007). In addition, fantasy film can imagine being stuck in time (*Groundhog Day*, 1993), or being able to rewind time at will (*Prince of Persia: The Sands of Time*, 2010).

And it might not be too much of a stretch to say that these stories can be understood at their most basic, fundamental level as variations on the 'coming of age' narrative (*Big*, 1988). Life is composed of a series of threshold 'coming of age' or 'rites of passage' moments: birth, childhood, puberty, the onset of sexual maturity, pregnancy, childbirth, ageing, and death. A central concern of fantasy therefore is the transitional stage of growing from a child into an adult and successfully negotiating one's place in the adult world. In order to complete this transition (transformation or metamorphosis) the individual needs to have confidence in their own ability to deal with life's challenges, so these threshold moments are explored and celebrated in tales that have the hero (whether child or adult, male or female) acquiring the skills necessary to overcome the monster, solve the puzzle, marry the prince/princess, survive the ordeal. The exceedingly common 'rags to riches' narrative is usually a variation on these themes, where the individual grows into their inheritance and therefore is in a position to deal with life. And even the ubiquitous battles of good against evil can be understood as a struggle to gain a mature adult control over the self.

The most common story type is the journey or quest (literal or metaphorical). Whether epic or heroic adventure, romance, or magical tale, a transformation occurs on the journey from home which marks the hero as having completed the inner transition from child to adult. The fantasy structure is modelled on this central narrative theme (departure, transformative trials, return). As in all stories, there is a change of state that supplies the narrative trajectory, but change in the fantasy story is often a profound transformation which not only involves an outward change, but also a journey inward that changes the hero's senses of identity and self. Curiously, despite often being set in an alternative domain where marvellous creatures may exist, and where the rules that organize our universe may not apply, we are able to recognize, in fantasy film, truths about ourselves and our world. Fantasy, the imaginary, the waking dream is then a fundamental part of the reality of human life.

2

THEORETICAL APPROACHES TO FANTASY IN FILM

This chapter is about theories of fantasy fiction and film. Issues of realism, narrative, psychoanalysis, feminism and adaptation are important sites of debate within film theory and criticism and an appreciation of their broad strokes is central to an appreciation of any fantasy film. These theoretical paradigms are borrowed from the related disciplines of literature and art, as film connects to other means of artistic expression and storytelling through language and image. In this chapter we directly address some of the ways that the notion of fantasy has impacted on the development of theory, the study of cinema and approaches to fantasy film.

We begin with the fantasy/realism debate. At first sight it may appear that fantasy is opposed to realism, but the section on fantasy and realism is actually concerned with a discussion of how the two are closely related and inter-dependent. The section on fantasy and narrative looks at the universality of fantasy storytelling, and demonstrates that regardless of the mode of telling – through oral tale, literary fantasy or fantasy film – they share common structures, characters, events and themes. Some theorists consider that in addition to these common elements fantasy, in whatever form, at whatever cultural moment, and from whatever social space, is shaped by a recurring pattern of archetypes that have powerful resonances for the human collective unconscious. We discuss these archetypes in the third section on psychoanalysis. Continuing the psychoanalytic theme into the section on fantasy and feminism, we then set out the importance of Jacques Lacan's (2001) notion of the mirror stage for film studies and the implications of gender representations in fantasy fiction and film. Finally, the section on fantasy adaptation introduces issues of fidelity and fandom, and the impact of new media forms, remediation and transmediation on contemporary fantasy film.

FANTASY AND REALISM

Some critics have made claims for the importance of realism (or mimesis) and its superiority relative to fantasy. Attitudes found in twentieth-century critical theory about the high status of realist art forms, compared to the relatively lowly status of fantasy art forms, can be traced back to Greek philosophers Plato and Aristotle and their writings on literature. In *Poetics* (fourth century BCE), Aristotle repeated the prevailing thought about art that at its highest level of achievement it 'imitates' nature (2008: 1–2). Kathryn Hume writes that to both Plato and his student Aristotle, 'literature was mimetic, and they analyzed only its mimetic components' (1984: 6). Hume continues by saying that 'insofar as their assumptions allowed them to recognize fantasy at all, they distrusted and disparaged it' (1984: 6). Aristotle measured the success of literature according to the probability or plausibility of its events and how realistically characters were drawn. Whereas realist drama received his approval, he condemned plays which used 'fantastic gimmicks' (Hume 1984: 6).

Following on from Aristotle's work in *Poetics* philosophers working in the tradition of Western aesthetics maintained that it is the goal of art to imitate nature. From the early Renaissance (fourteenth- to seventeenth-century Europe) up until the late nineteenth century, fine art, especially painting, tried to uphold this ideal. In literature, novelists such as Jane Austen, Honoré de Balzac, George Eliot and Leo Tolstoy also carried on this principle to faithfully represent nature and the social world. This conviction, that it was the role of art to reflect the world back to itself, gained fresh weight with the invention of photography and the movie camera. Siegfried Kracauer notes that the camera 'was unique in its ability to represent nature', and so 'If the ideal of art is to create an illusion of reality, the motion picture made it possible to achieve this ideal in an unprecedented way' (2004 [1960]: 135).

The invention of photography forced an opposition to develop between the realist tradition and the anti-realists who questioned the aims and role of art when the camera (and by extension the motion camera) is apparently able to achieve the imitation of reality with so little effort. The first wave of film theory in the 1930s was characterized, as Duncan Petrie says:

> by 'essentialist' positions on the cinema's true aesthetic vocation, such as those associated with the champion[s] of a realist aesthetic like Siegfried Kracauer [and André Bazin] on the one hand, and the anti-realist Rudolf Arnheim on the other.
>
> (1993: 2)

According to German scholar and film critic Kracauer (2004), film actually reproduces the raw material of external reality and is therefore able to show us our society and culture in a manner that enables us to understand and appreciate the world we live in. As a result, for Kracauer, it is the duty of film to record and reveal physical reality. André Bazin (2004 [1967]), influential critic, filmmaker, founder of film journal *Cahiers du Cinéma*, and champion of Italian Neorealism, also favoured an objective cinema. He argued that photography and film satisfy the drive towards realism in art because the object is reproduced through a mechanical process of re-presentation not subject to the interpretive intervention of the artist. For him, 'The objective nature of photography confers on it a quality of credibility absent from all other picture making' (Bazin 2004: 169).

Conversely, Rudolf Arnheim, film theorist and leading exponent of the anti-realist tradition, preferred a cinema that showed off its divergence from the 'real'. He said in an interview that 'art reveals to us the essence of things, the essence of our existence; that is its function' (Grundmann and Arnheim 2001). Arnheim believed that this revelatory quality of film is so innate that even if the filmmaker somehow managed to avoid any alteration of the original source object photographed, the very fact that the artist had intervened at all would always encourage the viewer to see the object differently. For example, the viewer might be encouraged to question the object's existence or its position in relation to other objects. For Arnheim it is this process of questioning that raises film to the status of art. If cinema were simply a mechanical reproduction of external reality it could not, according to Arnheim, be considered art at all.

Arnheim's opponent Kracauer was one of the first critics, but certainly not the last, to make connections between the realist/anti-realist debates and the first examples of filmmaking. He noted two opposing practices at work in film's very early days: one which concerned itself with recording real events, typified by the work of the Lumière brothers, and the other which explored film's potential for creative illusion, exemplified by Georges Méliès's 'trick' and fantasy films. The films made by the Lumière brothers have been seen as the forerunners of the documentary style of filmmaking. The brothers specialized in making short non-fiction 'actualité' films by setting up a static camera to record everyday events. Bill Nichols contends that films such as *Sortie des Usines Lumière à Lyon/Workers Leaving the Lumière Factory* (1895), that contain an 'underlying sense of authenticity' seem 'but a small step away from documentary film proper' (2001: 83). Nichols says that 'although they are but a single shot and last but a few minutes, they seem to provide a window onto the historical world' (2001: 83).

On the other hand Nichols says elsewhere that Méliès offered early film audiences 'a fantastic world unlike anything anyone had ever seen before', and they were drawn into 'a clearly fabricated world' (2010: 179). From this moment on, the 'illusion that what viewers see matches what they might see in their everyday world no longer pertains' (Nichols 2010: 179). Méliès's filmmaking style inaugurated a formalist (or expressionist) mode distinguishable by use of stylistic, expressionistic mise-en-scène which brings the telling of the story to the forefront. And it is in the telling of the story, in the stylistics, as well as in the type of story told, that fantasy is located in these films. Rather than representing reality the formalist film presents the artist's vision, and emphasizes technique and expressiveness. Contemporary formalists, such as Tim Burton and Terry Gilliam for example, in addition to making full use of the symbolic potential of mise-en-scène, also employ editing, lighting, sound, colour, and shot composition to augment the texture and meaning of the film's diegetic world. Nevertheless, as Louis Giannetti reminds us, 'Virtually all movie directors go to the photographable world for their subject matter, but what they do with this material – how they shape and manipulate it – is what determines their stylistic emphasis' (2005: 2). If the Lumière brothers' early films 'seemed to anchor the realist pole of cinema' (Nichols 2010: 179), then the descendants of Méliès's fantastic stories, and the descendants of his formalist style of filmmaking, can be seen throughout the modern fantastic, in spectacle-driven summer blockbusters, as well as in the more avant-garde art films of the surrealists.

Despite the fact that these two attitudes – realism: that art should convey reality, and formalism: that art can only become art by departing from reality – appear to be oppositional, it may not be helpful or entirely accurate to see formalism and realism as diametrically opposite. We should better see them as being in a complex relationship, as few individual films adopt either attitude exclusively. In order to understand this relationship we can revisit the diagram from Chapter 1 (Figure 1.5). 'Realism' and 'formalism' are positioned at either end of this continuum of film styles, and below that 'documentary' is placed at the extreme realism end, and 'avant-garde' at the extreme formalism end. Between realism and formalism is 'classicism', and between documentary and avant-garde is 'fiction'. In this way we can see that the classical style of narration sits between the other more extreme styles, and that the main concern of the classical style is to tell stories.

What we generally refer to as a realist style in fiction film is the system of narrative storytelling developed during Hollywood's classical period. The classical Hollywood continuity system sought narrative economy and a seamless style. Films were constructed so that the viewer was not aware of the construction. This method requires a complex system of visual codes to preserve the continuity of time and space, to maintain consistency of cause-and-effect relations, and to drive the plot forwards according to the principles of psychological realism (see Bordwell 1985: 156–204). Although post-classical films may depart to greater or lesser degrees from the continuity style, this style remains a standard of effective visual storytelling and one against which other forms tend to be measured.

Within the classical style of fictional storytelling we can identify aspects of the Lumière brothers' realist mode and aspects of Méliès's formalist, spectacle-driven mode. So far this discussion has been concerned with filmic style, which is about the manner in which a film tells its story (labelled variously plot, narrative or syuzhet). In some ways style may be seen as separable from content, but in other ways the two are closely connected. It is difficult, for example, to imagine a fantasy story about the quest of an epic hero who battles giants and dragons being told in a strictly documentary, realist style, and it is hard to imagine a film about the plight of an indigenous society being told in an avant-garde, formalist style. Certain genres will naturally tend to gather at a point, or at points, along the style continuum, and will be unlikely to be found at other points.

Most fantasy films, particularly popular blockbuster fantasy, combine classical narration and spectacle and therefore occupy the central portion of the continuum midway between the extremes of realism and formalism, but their exact positioning depends on their individual attitude towards realism and formalism. Whilst there will always be exceptions, fantasy films by formalist-style filmmakers like Ingmar Bergman and David Lynch, who employ expressive use of *mise-en-scène* and other symbolic visual codes, cluster together between classicism and formalism, whereas films by more realistically inclined fantasy filmmakers such as Steven Spielberg and George Lucas gather between classicism and realism. Seen in this way, classical realist aesthetics dominate the style of narrative filmmaking, even when the stories told are fantasy-based. We expect a certain amount of realism in the story events too. As Kathryn Fowkes points out, 'While it would be rare to hear that a movie was flawed because it was "too realistic," many are criticized for the opposite reason: "It was so unrealistic." "That could never happen." "It was implausible"' (2010: 4).

In practice there are three main types of fantasy setting, each with their own relationship to realism and the known world: (1) our everyday mundane world into which something magical has intruded (or which has been taken over by dream), (2) an alternative magical, self-contained secondary story world, or (3) a combination of the mundane world and a secondary world, where the story might begin in our everyday world and then the protagonist will happen upon a magical, fantasy space. Whatever the setting the audience will expect internal consistency (realism). If the everyday world is the setting, then apart from the intrusive magical elements everything else should look and sound authentic, as in *Harry Potter* (2001–2011). If a secondary world is the setting, then the look and sound of that world must be consistent with the rules according to which it operates. For example, Peter Jackson (2001–2003) faithfully realized J.R.R. Tolkien's mythical, medieval vision of Middle Earth, and the appearance of something from our modern life would violate the internal consistency of that world, and could be criticized for implausibility. And if a story begins in the known world then moves into a secondary world there will usually be some kind of portal or threshold space that defines the boundary between them. The portal or threshold will also therefore define the boundary between verisimilitude (likeness or resemblance to truth, reality, or fact) and vraisemblance (an internally consistent, believable diegetic world).

It is interesting that in his essay 'On Fairy-stories' Tolkien wrote disparagingly of any violation of the self-consistent integrity of the fantasy world by the introduction of inconsistent or contemporary elements. He said that, for him, escape into the land of Faërie was partly in response to what he saw as the ugliness and inhumanity of modern technology (Tolkien 1966: 82). And he singled out for particular condemnation the example of a modern street lamp (Figure 2.1), which his friend and colleague C.S. Lewis included as an anachronistic element in the landscape of Narnia (Tolkien 1966: 80). It was

Figure 2.1 Narnia's liminal street lamp in *The Chronicles of Narnia: The Lion, the Witch and the Wardrobe*

not until the publication of *The Magician's Nephew*, five years after the street lamp first appeared in *The Lion, the Witch and the Wardrobe*, that Lewis provided an explanation for its inclusion. In the meantime it remained a puzzling reminder in the secondary story world of the presence of the mundane primary world. Fowkes notes that though the lamp's appearance in the film version of *The Lion, the Witch and the Wardrobe* (2005) 'represents the anomalous intrusion of the primary world into the magical world' it also 'signals the potential interaction of the contemporary and the fantasy world' (2010: 151–2). She continues by saying that 'The lamp functions as a further transition from the wardrobe to the magical world and provides a landmark that lights the way back at the beginning of the film for Lucy' (Fowkes 2010: 152).

Its provenance notwithstanding, the lamp in the *Narnia* films (currently 2005–2010) and stories also functions as a rich metaphor. Its light has many potential symbolic readings: knowledge, wisdom, charity, spirituality, enlightenment, clarity, power, warmth, safety, guidance and love. In addition, as an element of the primary, real world, its anomalous, anachronistic presence beyond the threshold between the mundane world and Narnia may be used to understand a concept that Rosemary Jackson discusses in *Fantasy: The Literature of Subversion*, which is concerned with the relationship between fantasy and the real when the real is 're-placed and dis-located' (1998: 19). This concept is paraxis: 'that which lies alongside the main body' (Jackson 1998: 19). Jackson says that paraxis 'is a telling notion in relation to the place, or space, of the fantastic, for it implies an inextricable link to the main body of the "real" which it shades and threatens' (1998: 19). She borrows the term from optics, where:

> A paraxial region is an area in which light rays *seem* to unite at a point after refraction. In this area, object and image seem to collide, but in fact neither object nor reconstituted image genuinely reside there: nothing does.
>
> (Jackson 1998: 19, emphasis in original)

Jackson includes a diagram which is reproduced here (Figure 2.2). As a prefix, 'para' means 'side by side', and 'axis' is the 'central turning point' or

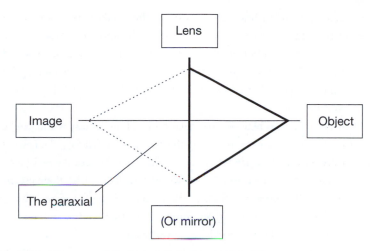

Figure 2.2   Diagram of the 'paraxial' (Jackson 1998: 19)

'central line'. So the paraxial is the threshold space between the real and the unreal where the divide between the two worlds is porous and indistinct.

Jackson employs the concept of the paraxial to illustrate how fantasy exists in the shadow of the real, and how a text will move from the mimetic, objective, realistic representation into a fantasy mode with a close relationship to the real. She says that 'fantasy re-combines and inverts the real, but it does not escape it: it exists in a parasitical or symbiotic relation to the real' (Jackson 1998: 20). This 'parasitical, symbiotic' relation of fantasy to the real is most clearly explained by Jackson when she states in an earlier passage that: 'Fantasy . . . has to do with inverting elements of this world, re-combining its constitutive features in new relations to produce something strange, unfamiliar and *apparently* "new", absolutely "other" and different' (1998: 8, emphasis in original).

The paraxial realm, then, lies in between the real and the fantasy space and so is the place where they meet and merge. It is also a useful visual metaphor for the way that the two worlds rely on one another. The real is a foil (to provide a foil is to set something off by contrast) for fantasy, and fantasy is a foil for the real. For example, the phenomenon of being able to fly on a winged horse is meaningless as fantasy without the knowledge that such flight is impossible in the real world. Fantasy worlds often make explicit and direct references to the everyday world that is left behind. In Chapter 1 we mentioned *The Wizard of Oz* (1939) where elements from Kansas get repeated in Oz, though they are strangely different, and also Tim Burton's Alice who finds elements repeated in Wonderland/Underland that she left behind her in the world above.

In this way the lens between the real world and the fantasy world can be seen to function as a mirror, reflecting the real into the fantasy, like Lewis's liminal street lamp, and also reflecting the fantasy back into the real (such as when characters return to the real world transformed by their escape into fantasy). Therefore we end our discussion of fantasy and realism by emphasizing that far from being oppositional, the two modes, and the two cinematic styles, like the two worlds, are always really held in close, symbiotic, proximity, and that in fact it is (almost) impossible to imagine one without the other.

FANTASY AND NARRATIVE

All fantasy is narrative. Disciplines that study narrative locate their historical roots in literary theory, which as mentioned in the previous section on Fantasy and Realism, dates back to the classical philosophers. But we need not go as far as that in this case, since contemporary narrative theory, or narratology, was strongly influenced by the structuralist movement of the 1960s, which was in turn influenced by the work of Ferdinand de Saussure (1857–1913) and Vladimir Propp (1895–1970).

Propp's (2009) work on the *Morphology of the Folktale*, first published in Russian in 1928, extended the Russian formalist approach to the study of folktale narratives, in which he looked for a common structure underlying this diverse group of stories. He distinguished 31 'functions' stemming from a character's actions, which he identified according to their significance within the narrative (Propp 2009: 20). This approach seems a reasonable one considering that the names of many folktale characters are simply nicknames that describe their role within the story; examples include 'Beauty' and the 'Beast', or the 'Frog King' (Carter 2008: 75). Propp also specified eight character types, and each of them potentially occupies a number of positions, which he called 'spheres of action', noting that each sphere of action might conversely be occupied by several different characters (2009: 85). These are not the psychologically motivated characters of classical film narration, but archetypes classified according to roles. Propp's seven spheres of action are:

1. The villain
2. The donor (provider)
3. The helper
4. The princess (a sought-for person) and her father
5. The dispatcher
6. The hero or victim
7. The false hero

(Propp 2009: 79–80)

As Graeme Turner explains in *Film as Social Practice*, all the character types in folktales fit within these seven spheres of action (2006: 99). Critics have 'demonstrated a degree of fit' between Propp's spheres of action and the characters in film (Turner 2006: 102), including fantasy film. For example, both Turner and Michael O'Shaughnessy and Jane Stadler, following Turner, mention how well they fit with the main characters in the original *Star Wars* (1977): the villain – Darth Vader; the donor – Ben Kenobi; the helper – Han Solo; the princess – Princess Leah; the dispatcher – R2D2; the hero – Luke Skywalker; the false hero – Darth Vader (O'Shaughnessy and Stadler 2002: 171; Turner 2006: 102).

Propp's characters carry out the functions (see below), which describe the folktale's plot. He argued that these functions are stable and constant elements 'independent of how and by whom they are fulfilled' (Turner 2006: 99). He also stated that the number of functions is limited to 31, though individual tales may not include them all. The order in which the functions occur is always the same (though some sequences may occur more than once in any one tale). He noted that all folktales have the same structure (Propp 2009: 19–24). Propp's functions (simplified) are:

1. Absentation: a member of a family leaves home (the hero is introduced).
2. Interdiction: an interdiction, prohibition or rule is addressed to the hero.
3. Violation of the interdiction: the interdiction/prohibition/rule is violated (the villain enters the tale).
4. Reconnaissance: the villain makes an attempt at reconnaissance.
5. Delivery: the villain gains information about the victim.
6. Trickery: the villain attempts to deceive the victim in order to take possession of the victim or the victim's belongings.
7. Complicity: the victim is taken in by deception, unwittingly helping the villain.
8. Villainy or Lack: the villain causes harm/injury to a family member. Alternatively, a member of the family lacks something or desires something.
9. Mediation: the injury/lack is made known. The hero is dispatched on a mission/quest.
10. Beginning counteraction: the hero agrees to, or decides upon a counteraction.
11. Departure: the hero leaves home.
12. First function of the donor: the hero is tested and receives a magical agent or a helper (donor).
13. Hero's reaction: the hero reacts to actions of the future donor.
14. Receipt of a magical agent: the hero acquires use of a magical agent.
15. Guidance: the hero is transferred to the location of the object of the quest.
16. Struggle: the hero and the villain engage in direct combat.
17. Branding: the hero is branded (wounded or marked).
18. Victory: the villain is defeated.
19. Liquidation: the initial misfortune or lack is resolved.
20. Return: the hero returns.
21. Pursuit: the hero is pursued.
22. Rescue: the hero is rescued from pursuit.

23. Unrecognized arrival: the hero arrives home or in another country unrecognized.
24. Unfounded claims: a false hero makes false claims.
25. Difficult task: the hero is set a difficult task.
26. Solution: the task is completed.
27. Recognition: the hero is recognized.
28. Exposure: the false hero/villain is exposed.
29. Transfiguration: the hero is given a new appearance.
30. Punishment: the villain is punished.
31. Wedding: the hero marries and ascends the throne (is rewarded).

(Adapted from Propp 2009: 25–65, and Turner 2006: 100–1)

Turner and others identify that Propp's structure comprises six stages (see O'Shaughnessy and Stadler 2002: 171; Turner 2006: 100–1). Functions 1 to 7 are labelled 'Preparation'; 8 to 10: 'Complication'; 11 to 15: 'Transference'; 16 to 19: 'Struggle'; 20 to 26: 'Return', and 27 to 31: 'Recognition'. This formal organization is noteworthy because it emphasizes that even though we might not so readily recognize some of Propp's more specific and prescriptive functions, it is easy enough to apply his overarching structure to a great many fantasy film narratives.

In his introduction to the second edition of *Morphology of the Folktale*, Alan Dundes comments on the 'enormous impact Propp's study has had on folklorists, linguists, anthropologists, and literary critics' (2009: xi). In particular, Dundes mentions Claude Lévi-Strauss, who examined the role of myths in primitive cultures. Whilst Propp directed his attention to the narrative structure of tales, Lévi-Strauss (1978) was interested in how stories reveal the particular conditions of their production and exchange, and how these conditions transformed their common structures. He also noted, however, that despite their individual differences, all primitive narratives and cultural myths served the same function for their society: as a kind of guidebook on to how to live their lives. Turner explains the function of myth in this way:

Within myths, contradictions and inequities which could not be resolved in the real world were resolved symbolically. The function of myth was to place those contradictions – between humans and his [*sic*] natural environment, for instance, or between life and death – as part of natural existence. Myths negotiated a peace between men and women and their environment so that they could live in it without agonizing over its frustrations and cruelties.

(2006: 103)

Therefore, as Turner notes, 'the notion . . . that narrative makes sense of the world . . . is explicit in myth and ritual' (2006: 103). What is compelling is that Lévi-Strauss's work emphasizes the universality of the tradition of creating fantasy stories as an innate practice of human beings. Whilst individual myths and customs may be the expression of specific cultures, they hold important and fundamental structures in common, and can be seen as evidence of the great importance of the world of story.

An example of the fundamental structures held in common by myth according to Lévi-Strauss is his work on binary oppositions, which reveals the influence of Saussurean linguistics on structural anthropology. Saussure's (1916) linguistics focus on the rules of language, and stress that a signifier (word) sits in relation to all other signifiers that it differs from. Saussure made a distinction between language as it is used (*parole*) and the rules regarding its use (*langue*). This distinction is a useful way to think about a number of systems that operate according to a general set of rules (*langue*), but that are subject to individual interpretation (*parole*). Lévi-Strauss, along with other structuralist thinkers such as Lacan, made connections between Saussure's work and systems such as kinship, the unconscious, and films, which can be said to behave like a language in that each speech act tells us something about the individual speaker as language use is dynamic and contextual. The separation between *langue* and *parole* might be used, for instance, to account for the way that genres evolve.

In Chapter 1 we thought about the fantasy genre as a series of fuzzy sets with a central definitive film surrounded by other films that share a greater or lesser set of characteristics in common. An alternative to this model is to think about the relationship that each fantasy film (*parole*/speech act) has to the wider generic rules (*langue*). Each film interprets the rules that govern the genre/subgenre or fuzzy set in its own idiosyncratic way whilst bearing a relationship to the overarching genre that operates like a language (see Schatz 2003). A film is made by selecting (and rejecting) individual elements (words) such as setting, iconography, and character, Proppian sphere of action or function, and rules such as the conventions of structure.

Lévi-Strauss argued that myth also works like a language, as a complex system of relations between elements or terms, and that all human culture is governed by a system of binary opposites where each of these terms sits in relation to what it is not. The terms are held in conflict – such as male/female, strong/weak, raw/cooked, nature/culture (Lévi-Strauss 1969). Meaning therefore is, as Turner puts it, 'a product of the construction of differences and similarities; in this case, placing an object on one side of an opposition rather than on the other' (2006: 104). For Lévi-Strauss any narrative is a continual creation of binary oppositions which, being in conflict, propel the narrative towards the final goal that is the resolution of conflict. Fantasy film narrative is often driven forward by a series of binary conflicts, for example around central characters such as the hero and the villain, symbolic elements such as darkness and light, or moral categories such as good and evil. The significance of this system of binary analysis for fantasy film is returned to later when we consider the notion of archetypes (which are often paired: masculine/feminine, persona/shadow), and feminist theory, because gender difference is commonly identified through binaries (active/passive). Meanwhile we continue this section on narrative by looking at Tzvetan Todorov's work on story structure.

Todorov's narratological methodology, set out in *Poetics of Prose* (1977), is influenced by Saussure, Roland Barthes (1990 [1970]) and Propp, and also refers to *Poetics* in which Aristotle stated that a plot should have a 'beginning, a middle, and an end' (2008: 14). Todorov's revision is that:

> The minimal completed plot consists in the passage from one equilibrium to another. An 'ideal' narrative begins with a stable situation which is disturbed by some power or force. There results a state of disequilibrium; by the action of a force directed in the opposite direction, the equilibrium is re-established; the second equilibrium is similar to the first, but the two are never identical.
>
> (1977: 111)

This structure can be compared to Lévi-Strauss's model of narrative being a succession of conflict and the resolution of conflict, and also to David Bordwell's summary of the '"canonical" story format' which follows the 'introduction of setting and characters – explanation of a state of affairs – complicating action – ensuing events – outcome – ending' (1985: 35). Whilst Todorov notes that narratives do not need to present story information in a linear order, he says that the pattern (equilibrium – disequilibrium – re-equilibrium) is nevertheless present in all plots.

In common with Propp and Todorov, Joseph Campbell's (1993 [1949]) work also 'describes general, recurring patterns in all forms of story-telling' (O'Shaughnessy and Stadler 2002: 170). Campbell's approach differs from Propp's, however, in that whereas Propp was only interested in defining the underlying structure of tales, Campbell goes on to explicate the implications of the common structures. Like Lévi-Strauss, Campbell seeks to understand 'the role and meanings of myths and stories in human society' (O'Shaughnessy and Stadler 2002: 171), but his particular approach is informed by the discipline of psychoanalysis, notably the work of Carl Jung (1875–1961), student of Sigmund Freud (1856–1939). Rather than being concerned only with the nature of the individual story, Campbell's approach, because of its basis in psychoanalysis, focuses on the meanings, relevance and significance that the story holds for the audience.

FANTASY AND PSYCHOANALYSIS

The term 'fantasy' takes on another meaning in psychoanalysis, which is that of a psychological process that has particular value and function for the individual, tied to their life experience, desires, hopes, fears, anxieties and aspirations. Psychoanalytic theory has significance for the study of fantasy film for a number of reasons. First, it enables us to think about the power of a medium that plays on spectatorial pleasure. Second, it links fantasy as a mental process to films which offer fantasy scenarios that can be compared to dreams. Third, psychoanalysis allows us to make associations between myth and fantasy film because it consolidates the idea of universal fantasies that find their way into our lives through popular story forms. Finally, Campbell's psychoanalytically-informed work suggests that films may be telling us the same kinds of stories that we tell ourselves in dreams, thereby linking psychoanalysis to film, allowing us to see film functioning as a collective dream.

In psychoanalysis conscious fantasies include imagined ideas, such as daydreams, that express something of our fictions, desires or aims, including sexual feelings. Freud understood fantasy to be fundamental to the lives of human beings, and to emerge in the imaginative play of children, in day-dreams and in the creative activities of people of all ages. He believed that the analysis of fantasies could reveal a great deal about the mental and emotional workings of his therapeutic subjects. Within Freudian psychoanalysis, the unconscious is a storehouse of ideas, memories, feelings, and urges that, though existing outside our conscious awareness, nevertheless continue to exert a powerful influence on our actions and opinions throughout life. Some writers differentiate the kinds of conscious fantasies that we are at least partly aware of, and those that reside within the unconscious part of the personality, by spelling the latter with a 'ph' (see Laplanche and Pontalis 2006 [1973]; Steiner 2003). Phantasies emerge (in dreams for instance), and merge with fantasy, connecting to an individual's unconscious, yet constituting a protective barrier to this central core of the personality (see Freud 1991).

Freud used the plot of the play *Oedipus Rex* by the classical Greek writer Sophocles (fifth century BCE), to elucidate his theories around the unconscious human incestuous desires towards the parent of the opposite sex and murderous impulses towards the parent of the same sex. His ideas eventually coalesced into the 'Oedipus Complex' (see Freud 1990: 448–9). Elsewhere, in 'Creative Writers and Day-Dreaming', Freud explored the relationship between a writer's work and their fantasy/phantasy lives, making explicit connections between conscious and unconscious fantasy as defined within psychoanalysis, and individual acts of story creation (1990: 129–41). This concern with the associations between stories and the human psyche links the psychoanalysis of Freud with Campbell's approach to narrative, but Campbell is consumed by the study of the collective implications rather than significance for any particular individual.

In the preface to his book *The Hero with a Thousand Faces* Campbell writes that his purpose is to dig down into the symbolism of traditional stories of a wide range of different societies in order to divine their universal meanings and uncover, using psychoanalysis, 'the basic truths by which man [sic] has lived throughout the millenniums of his [sic] residence on the planet' (1993: viii). Campbell is interested in a universal story motif which collates the similarities, rather than any manifest differences, to be found across myths, legends and religious practices, and he says that he is able to detect a dominant pattern or structure. In his view it is almost impossible to overestimate the importance of these myths and legends for the development, continued progress and wellbeing of human beings because every fantasy-based story, even 'the smallest nursery fairy tale', contains symbols that are 'spontaneous productions of the psyche' (Campbell 1993: 4).

Campbell developed his ideas about the organization of stories out of the psychological theories of Jung. Originally a colleague of Freud, Jung (1964) adapted the Freudian model of the human psyche and blended it with his own extensive research into philosophy, religion and mythology. In place of the Freudian structure of the human personality (id, ego and superego, ranged across the unconscious and conscious areas of the psyche), Jung's schema named the conscious, the personal unconscious and the collective unconscious (which he later renamed the objective psyche). An important element for fantasy story is the collective unconscious, which Jung saw as comprising shared ideas and archetypes common to all people. Ideas contained in the collective unconscious emerge into the personal unconscious as dreams (which can then be interpreted by someone with knowledge and understanding of the universal symbols), and then out into the external world through concepts and ideas expressed in art, literature and film, images being especially important.

Certainly, Luke Hockley describes Jungian psychology as a 'psychology of images' (2001: 1). He says that 'For Jung, images encapsulate the totality of a psychological situation, both the aspects that are conscious, and the elements that are unconscious', also commenting that 'images encourage . . . psychological reflection' and 'initiate a personal response' (Hockley 2001: 3). Understood in this way viewed images communicate directly with images residing in the unconscious, connecting with its concerns and speaking in its language in a way that feels significant and particular to each individual.

A fundamental component of the language of the collective unconscious identified by Jung is the archetype.

Archetypes are primordial, archaic images, 'forms without content' and 'through the collective unconscious, the human is able to tap into these inherited forms and experience perceptions common to every member of the species' (Iaccino 1998: xi). James Iaccino describes archetypes as '"racial memories" which unknowingly shape and mold our current thought processes', and which 'have found expression in tribal lore, mythology, fairy tales, religious systems and primitive art' (1998: xi). Moreover, Hockley describes the role of the archetype as being to provide guidance at key stages and to 'regulate the life-long process of psychological growth that analytical psychology terms the individuation processes' (2001: 31). In fantasy film the individuation process is referenced in any 'rites of passage' or 'coming of age' plot that deals with trials to be overcome which result in some kind of transformation, new beginning, or re-equilibrium, which describes most fantasy films, but some recent examples include the Harry Potter series, The Chronicles of Narnia, The Golden Compass (2007), Twilight (2008), and How to Train Your Dragon (2010).

Iaccino notes that Jungian archetypes are not 'fully developed pictures', but a kind of featureless form that represents 'the possibility of a certain type of perception and action' (1998: xi). Each archetype controls our psyche 'via particular situations in life that can be directly tied to the collective form' (Iaccino 1998: xii). It is not surprising then that Jung's list of archetypes includes the Mother and Father and the Child archetypes; the Persona and Shadow archetypes; the Anima/Animus archetypes; the Fairytale archetypes, such as those of the Hero, the Wise Old Man, the Trickster, the Maiden or Princess, and the Animal (see Jung 2010 [1959]). Each archetype has the potential for both good and evil aspects. The Mother archetype may be represented as a benign earth mother, a fertility goddess, or a maternal well, but also as a devouring, punishing mother, whilst the Father archetype may be represented as a fair leader, a protector, and a kind monarch, or as a corrupt tyrant, despot, or evil lord.

Campbell took these featureless forms and mapped them on to a universe of story where archetypes find individual expression and audience specificity.

The universal story motif that Campbell identifies as a result is the 'one, shape-shifting yet marvelously constant story' that is the 'adventure of the hero', which he says is a 'magnification of the formula represented in the rites of passage', and which we identified in Chapter 1 as a plot type common to very many fantasy stories (1993: 3, 30). The purpose of the original rituals enacted throughout human history was to 'conduct people across those difficult thresholds of transformation that demand a change in the patterns not only of conscious but also of unconscious life' (Campbell 1993: 10). These rites of passage, which Campbell describes as 'ceremonials of birth, naming, puberty, marriage, burial, etc.', involve 'exercises of severance . . . from the stage being left behind', followed by a period of 'enacted rituals' symbolic of the new life stage being prepared for, and finally, rebirth back into the normal world (1993: 10). Such ceremonials follow the structure of 'separation-initiation-return', which is, for Campbell, echoed and repeated in the 'nuclear unit of the monomyth', and which he summarizes:

> A hero ventures forth from the world of common day into a region of supernatural wonder: fabulous forces are there encountered and a decisive victory is won: the hero comes back from this mysterious adventure with the power to bestow boons on his fellow man.
>
> (1993: 30)

The monomyth involves 'situation archetypes' such as Quest, Initiation, Fall, and Death and Rebirth, which are organized into the 17 separate stages of the hero's journey as set out in Table 2.1, where we have also included notes about any relevant Jungian character and situation archetypes, along with, where possible, an illustration from The Lord of the Rings film trilogy.

The Jungian explanation why stories featuring these archetypal figures resonate so strongly is that, as they originate from the universal collective unconscious, they are psychologically 'true' for us, even when the worlds they inhabit and the problems they face are apparently impossible according to the rules of our everyday, waking lives. In addition to the seemingly fundamental truth of the cast list, the stories deal symbolically with universal emotions such as love, hate, passion, and envy, and threshold moments like birth, puberty,

Table 2.1 Campbell's monomyth, Jung's archetypes and The Lord of the Rings film trilogy

Stages of the monomyth	Jungian character and situation archetypes	Illustration from The Lord of the Rings
1. Departure		
The Call to Adventure: A sign that some change is coming for the character(s).	The Hero (the Self symbol), representative of the emerging ego, begins the journey towards individuation (spiritual, psychological or emotional maturity).	Frodo is visited by Gandalf and told that he must prepare to leave with the Ring.
Refusal of the Call: 'Refusal of the summons converts the adventure into its negative' (Campbell 1993: 59).	There is resistance to the work of individuation.	Frodo repeatedly denies that he is the right person to deal with the matter of the Ring.
Supernatural Aid: 'The first encounter of the hero-journey is with a protective figure' (Campbell 1993: 69).	The Wise Old Man or Woman. 'The early weakness of the hero is balanced by the appearance of strong "tutelary" figures' (Henderson 1964: 101).	Gandalf sends Frodo on his Quest.
The Crossing of the First Threshold: 'The hero goes forward in his adventure until he comes to the "threshold guardian" at the entrance to the zone of magnified power' (Campbell 1993: 77).	Threshold Guardians. Each stage of the journey of the Self is negotiated by dealing with various obstacles.	Sauron's Ringwraiths attack Frodo on the borders of The Shire. Further threshold guardians include the Balrog of Moria, and Shelob who guards the route into Mordor.

Table 2.1 Continued

Stages of the monomyth	Jungian character and situation archetypes	Illustration from The Lord of the Rings
The Belly of the Whale: The hero, once past the threshold, 'is swallowed into the unknown' (Campbell 1993: 90), which is the place where s/he is tested.	The unknown regions stand symbolically for the unconscious mind, for example, the dream world, where internal battles rage between the Self and the Shadow selves.	The land of Middle Earth beyond The Shire where Frodo faces many trials, endures symbolic and almost literal death, and where he attains mature heroic adulthood.
2. Initiation		
The Road of Trials: The hero continues on the quest and is tested.	Characters encountered here represent the 'shadow selves' and these archetypes must be battled and overcome and/or assimilated.	Gollum/Sméagol is one of Frodo's shadow selves, whilst Gandalf's list of shadow selves includes the Balrog, Saruman and Sauron.
The Meeting with the Goddess: She stands for 'mother, sister, mistress, bride . . . the incarnation of the promise of perfection' (Campbell 1993: 111).	Jung's 'anima' archetype is an image of the female in the male psyche, or the feminine aspect of the female self.	Galadriel is an example of this archetype. We see both light and dark at work in her character once Frodo offers her the Ring as her resolve is tested and she does battle with and defeats her shadow self (Figure 2.3).
Woman as the Temptress: This archetype symbolizes any temptation that offers the hero an easy or short-term answer to his/her	Like other Jungian archetypes, the anima is ambiguous, capable of both good and bad actions.	Galadriel represents the figure of 'The Woman as Temptress', testing Frodo by offering him a chance to rid himself of the burden of the ring.

problems or creates a distraction from their main goal.		
Atonement with the Father: A climactic confrontation with a being of immense power.	The ultimate transformative battle to overcome (repress or assimilate into experience) the overwhelming shadow self.	Frodo defeats Sauron by sending the Ring into the fires of Mount Doom, almost dying himself as a result.
Apotheosis: After defeating the enemy there is a time of bliss, joy and celebration.	The transformation of the self signalled symbolically through images of death and rebirth.	The Fellowship witness Mordor's collapse, Frodo hallucinates the Shire and the two hobbits prepare for death.
The Ultimate Boon: This is the prize that was the goal of the hero's quest.	Individuation is achieved.	Frodo's quest has brought the boon of peace to Middle Earth.
3. Return		
Refusal of the Return: 'When the hero-quest has been accomplished . . . the adventurer still must return with his life-transmuting trophy. . . . But the responsibility has been frequently refused' (Campbell 1993: 193).		Not applicable.
The Magic Flight: 'If the trophy has been attained against . . . opposition . . . then the last stage of the mythological round becomes a lively, often comical, pursuit' (Campbell 1993: 196–7).		Not applicable.

Table 2.1 Continued

Stages of the monomyth	Jungian character and situation archetypes	Illustration from The Lord of the Rings
Rescue from Without: 'The hero may have to be brought back from his [sic] supernatural adventure by assistance from without. That is to say, the world may have to come and get him' (Campbell 1993: 207).		Frodo and Sam's rescue from Mount Doom by Gandalf and the great eagles.
The Crossing of the Return Threshold: 'The hero adventures out of the land we know into darkness; there he accomplishes his adventure . . . and his return is described as a coming back . . .' (Campbell 1993: 217).		Frodo is reborn as a hero before whom all races of Middle Earth bow down at Aragorn's crowning which heralds 'The Days of the King'.
Master of the Two Worlds: 'Freedom to pass back and forth across the world division' (Campbell 1993: 229).		Not found literally in The Lord of the Rings. Frodo is unable to settle in The Shire and finally journeys with Bilbo and the elves to the Grey Havens and from there to Valinor in the west.
Freedom to Live: The hero enjoys the life he has won.	Having achieved individuation and integration of archetypal forms the ego finds peace.	Sam, Merry and Pippin happily live out their lives in the Shire.

Figure 2.3   Galadriel as shadow archetype in *The Lord of the Rings: The Fellowship of the Ring*

marriage, parenthood, death, and the afterlife. Each time the story is told, however, it is made anew by the teller to appeal to the concerns and tastes of each individual audience and adapted to the particularities of each socio-cultural, historical context, and this is why Campbell describes his hero as having 'a thousand faces'. His work on the monomyth has had a large impact on fantasy filmmaking. Indeed, a number of filmmakers have acknowledged their debt to him, including Lucas, who used this structure in the making of *Star Wars*. Spielberg, Francis Ford Coppola and John Boorman, among others, display the value and versatility of the hero's quest narrative.

Christopher Vogler's screenwriting manual *The Writer's Journey: Mythic Structure for Writers* (2007) is explicitly based on Campbell's monomyth, and Jung's depth psychology, which Vogler relates and applies to contemporary story-telling, explaining how to construct stories about heroes on mythic quests. But film fantasy means more than simply stories about questing heroes, and it is worth mentioning that the process of fantasy is just as important as the fantasy content. In fact, Jean Laplanche and Jean-Bertrand Pontalis's notion that 'Fantasy . . . is not the object of desire, but its setting' (1986: 26) led Elizabeth Cowie to make an explicit connection with film. She says that 'while on the one hand fantasy can be characterized as a series of wishes presented through imaginary happenings, on the other hand it is also a structure: fantasy as the *mise-en-scène* of desire' (Cowie 1993: 147). This statement summarizes the role that cinema plays in presenting the spectator with a site where their fantasies and desires can be explored. It suggests that it is not simply that cinema offers fantasy narratives, but also that the cinema itself, the screen, the characters, the situations, the spaces, the temporalities, the fluidity of identification allowed, make up the pleasure of film for the spectator (Thornham 1997: 95).

FANTASY AND FEMINISM

Cinema's fantasy narratives not only reflect society's dreams, but social reality too. This combination of dream and reality emerges in the psychoanalytical work of Freud, Jung, Lacan and Campbell, who all in some way report on, uphold and perpetuate conservative, misogynist notions of gender representation. For example, phallocentric psychoanalysis based on Freudian theory explains femininity as lack, as silent, castrated and passive, a kind of negative image of masculinity, and as 'other'. Indeed, in her feminist reading of Lacan, Elizabeth Grosz comments that 'psychoanalysis itself is . . . phallocentric in its perspectives, methods and assumptions', and she says that 'Relations between psychoanalysis and women have always been, and remain . . . highly ambivalent and fraught with difficulties' (1990: 3–6). Despite this, many feminist film theorists have engaged with psychoanalysis in the project to address misogyny inherent in the social world and the media it produces.

Regardless of gender, we are all subjects embedded in a pre-existing language structure which produces and maintains things by naming them. Traditionally, within a patriarchal culture, men have inevitably been in charge of the creation and application of language, and as a result patriarchal power is naturally encoded into the language with which we all write, speak and imagine. The kinds of stories we hear and see, the ways these stories play out, and the ways in which they are transmitted, shape our beliefs and attitudes, and these get fed back into the stories we ourselves make. One aim of feminist theory, therefore, has been to challenge the notion of the subject (the self, the social being) by exploring the politics of representation to reveal how texts and the language they are built from work to uphold the existing social structures, which, in the Anglo-American corner of the Western world at least, are organized around gender hierarchies and the primacy of white, Protestant, male heterosexuals.

In Chapter 1 we considered how fantasy might perform a liberatory function as it may encourage us to question established norms, and in the previous sections we have suggested that fantasy film plays a key role in connecting modern audiences to timeless images, archetypes and narratives of the collective unconscious. It is also important though to recognize fantasy film's potential part in the perpetuation of repressive, conservative ideas, such as those around gender roles, not least because of the influential role fantasy plays in the lives of children and young adults, in other words, those who are learning how to view the world and their place in it. An individual's identity is achieved by internalizing the discourses that surround them from birth, and Lacan's (2001) notion of the mirror stage, which has a significant place in film theory, explicates this process of internalization.

Lacan's work in general involves a consideration of how the 'social is placed within the individual and, in turn, how the individual is positioned within the social' (Ragland-Sullivan 1992: 202). In his concept of the mirror stage Lacan (2001) describes the situation of a baby first seeing its own image in a mirror. This moment is assumed to occur when the child is between 6 and 18 months old and therefore at a stage when s/he is 'in a state of powerlessness and motor incoordination', and during which 'the infant anticipates on an imaginary plane the apprehension and mastery of its bodily unity [. . .] which it still objectively lacks' (Laplanche and Pontalis 2006: 250–1). The mirror stage, for Lacan, thus 'marks a first stage in the child's acquisition of an identity independent of the mother, the genesis of a sense of self or personal unity, the origin of the child's sexual drives and the first process of social acculturation' (Grosz 1990: 32). For all of these things to happen the baby has to recognize and identify with the mirror image. Therefore this stage can be read as a metaphor for how an individual constructs their selfhood from that which is reflected back to them in intersocial relations, including media such as film. Of particular interest for our analysis of filmic representations is that the stage can also be seen as a metaphor for identification with on-screen characters, and the role this plays in the construction of identity.

Not only is this mirror stage a moment of reflected self image, but also of the origin of the ideal ego, as the child sees a 'visual, corporal unity . . . in contrast to the tumult felt within . . . In this sense, the mirror stage presents a state of anticipatory unity', but is also a 'metaphor for the alienation that first forms the ego from the outside world through identification with others' (Ragland-Sullivan 1986: 275). This symbolic moment is significant for the generation of gender identity because it embodies how human beings shape their sense of self through identifying with others, identifying with reflections of how society sees them, and identification with an ideal ego, a better version of themselves to aspire to. All of these mechanisms are available through film, the role models presented and the reflections given back to individuals of their status in culture and the social world.

According to Lacan (2001) individuals come to recognize their place in society and what is appropriate and acceptable behaviour through rules generated by the symbolic (or social) order and transmitted via language. Both genders receive the raw materials of identity in the same way, but the role models and reflections offered share very few similarities. Ellie Ragland-Sullivan says that 'The "enemy" which feminists must confront . . . is neither class structure nor patriarchy per se, but the mimetic mirror-stage process of fusion and difference by which the human subject takes on its nuclear form' (1986: 269). This ongoing process of an independence of identity can be compared to Jung and Campbell's notion of individuation already discussed, a process – aided by reading or watching fantasy scenarios where symbolic individuation (rites of passage) are played out – through which a person achieves a place in the social world and a sense of self as an adult.

The 'stage', then, becomes the ongoing state of subjectivity through which the ego forms as a result of the processes of identification with the image (ideal ego). The notion of the image can be widened to include a number of ways in which individuals may see themselves reflected back from the mirror of society and culture. For example, Christian Metz acknowledges the role of cinema in identity formation when he writes that 'film is like the mirror' in the mirror stage (Metz 1982: 45; Easthope 1993: 12–13). Therefore we will now consider some examples of the kinds of images women see reflected back to them in fantasy – and consequently what constitutes the raw materials from which they might construct their identities.

We established in Chapter 1 that traditional stories (myth, legend, folklore, fairy tale) form the main ingredients of the 'ocean of story' from which much contemporary fantasy draws its inspiration for stories, themes and character types (Clute and Grant 1997: 704). These traditional stories inevitably have a polarized, binary view of gender. For example, American feminists argue that 'fairy tales shape our cultural values and understanding of gender roles by invariably depicting women as wicked, beautiful, and passive, while portraying men, in absolute contrast, as good, active, and heroic' (Haase 2004: 3). Indeed, if fairy tales' heroines are vulnerable and long-suffering their villains are often cruel female characters (such as bad mothers, nagging wives, wicked witches and sadistic stepmothers, evil fairies and ogresses), capable of monstrous acts. In 'Ashypet', the Brothers Grimm's (1812) version of 'Cinderella', for instance, the stepsisters' mother hands her daughters a knife with the instruction to mutilate their feet (one to cut off a big toe, and the other, part of her heel) in order to fit the cast-off slipper and so marry the prince (Grimm and Grimm 2005: 83).

Marina Warner comments that such 'figures of female evil stride through the best-loved classic fairy tales' (1995: 201), though she also says that it is the contribution by Disney's *Snow White and the Seven Dwarfs* (1937) and *Cinderella* (1949), which have done more than any other creation to naturalize female – maternal – malignancy in the imaginations of children worldwide' (1995: 207). Warner writes that 'Both films concentrate with exuberant glee on the towering, taloned, raven-haired wicked stepmother' (Figure 2.4) and that 'all Disney's powers of invention failed to save the princes from featureless banality and his heroines from saccharin sentimentality' (1995: 207). In the 'Cinderella' story (including the Disney version) we find the latent message that the overall goal for a girl who wishes to secure herself a happy ending is to find a Prince. Indeed, her social status, her entire happiness (and possibly her very life), is contingent upon pleasing him (satisfying his requirements) sufficiently so that he will marry her.

Fairy tales are often dominated by women's concerns, and all traditional happy endings that feature a young woman involve her not only finding but

Figure 2.4   The wicked queen's magic mirror in *Snow White and the Seven Dwarfs*

marrying the Prince. For boys, especially in male-focused myth, the adventure may involve leaving home to do battle with the monster, transforming into a great hero (who is brave, clever, a skilled warrior), being recognized as hero and being rewarded. So traditionally whilst heroes go off to fight the dragons, monsters or demons that threaten the world of men, their women wait patiently at home to be freed from danger before becoming the prize awarded to the conquering hero, which signals his triumphant entry into the adult world and sexuality.

This might suggest that traditional stories have always unproblematically supported the prevailing ideology, but this is not necessarily so. It is possible to find instances of resistance and tension. The story of 'Beauty and the Beast' can be used to demonstrate such a struggle. This fairy tale is about a failed merchant father and his lovely daughter, Beauty, whom he agrees to hand over to a wealthy but apparently hideous half-human creature, the Beast, in order to redeem his own life. Beauty willingly sacrifices her happiness for her father's safety and agrees to live with Beast. She eventually grows to love him. Her love breaks the spell under which Beast was living and brings about his transformation back into a handsome prince, and the two live happily ever after. The story exists in many oral and literary forms as well as dozens of film versions, including Disney's in 1991 and Jean Cocteau's in 1946.

Cocteau's surrealist fantasy is based on the version of the fairy tale written by Madame Leprince de Beaumont (1756), a French governess working in England. The story's subtextual reference is arranged marriages, where women were passed from father to husband, usually as part of a financial settlement, with little or no regard for the woman's views on her fate. Beaumont's version encourages the bride, as cultural historian Christopher Frayling comments in the DVD extras, to 'make the best of a bad job'. Frayling says that Beaumont's version argues that 'It may seem that your arranged marriage is to a bestial man, but when you get to know him better, with a little bit of encouragement and patience, maybe it will turn into a good marriage after all'. This is a story that thereby works to organize women's lives in a way that will benefit men's social systems. The earlier, seventeenth-century version by Madame de Villeneuve, however, was part of a radical attempt by 'women of letters' to add 'their voices to . . . cautionary tales . . . through an overt infusion of feminism, and reworking oral sources to decry arranged marriages and stifling gender roles for women' (Lim 2005: 167). In using Beaumont's conservative version, Cocteau's treatment of the story ignores any sense of Villeneuve's radicalism, or the female perspective and, as Frayling notes in the DVD commentary, objectifies Beauty, moulding her:

> into an artefact. The emotional centre of the film is the Beast rather than Beauty and it is not told from the woman's point of view, as a *rites de passage.* It is very much told from a male film director's point of view.

Both the story and the way it is told by Cocteau sets Beauty up as a thing to be looked at. Beast's castle is populated with surreal life: candelabra held up by real, apparently disembodied arms, and full-sized 'sculptures' that are actors covered with paint. In Beast's castle Cocteau's Beauty becomes a living statue who acts only according to the desires, fantasies or needs of the male characters. She initially leaves home to save her father and she ornaments Beast's castle because he desires it, her purpose being only to be looked at. When she sees (though a magic mirror) that her father is ill she goes to him, returning to Beast when she sees (through the same mirror) that he is ill because she is not there with him. This is the kind of representation that prompted early feminist film theorists to interrogate the way that cinema reproduces social power relations, by asking questions such as: 'Whose desire is at work in a particular film?', 'Whose unconscious is being addressed?' (Kaplan 2000: 2).

The aim of such criticism was that 'of transforming not only film theory and criticism, but also hierarchically gendered social relations in general' (Stam 2000: 170). Laura Mulvey's 1975 essay 'Visual Pleasure and Narrative Cinema' used 'Psychoanalytic theory . . . as a political weapon, demonstrating the way the unconscious of patriarchal society has structured film form' (1989: 14). Although it subsequently attracted criticism (some of it her own), at the time of publication Mulvey's essay broke new ground and generated a great deal of debate. In it she revealed cinema's 'unconscious mechanisms related to the construction of images, erotic ways of looking, audience identification, and the Hollywood editing style' (Erens 1990: 3). Though Mulvey was writing explicitly about classical Hollywood narration her critique might apply equally well to Cocteau's La Belle et la Bête/Beauty and the Beast.

In her essay Mulvey employs a number of binary opposites to argue that 'In a world ordered by sexual imbalance, pleasure in looking has been split between active/male and passive/female' (1989: 19). She states that in narrative film women are positioned in order to 'connote to-be-looked-at-ness', a passive object of erotic spectacle (Mulvey 1989: 19, emphasis in original). Men control the gaze, which is always active, and always male, whether it is that of the camera, the characters looking at one another, or that of the spectator. Robert Stam summarizes that 'Women spectators had the Hobson's Choice of identifying either with the active male protagonist or with the passive, victimized female antagonist' (2000: 174). For Mulvey, mainstream cinema replicates patriarchal social conventions by privileging the male in terms of narrative and spectacle. She says that 'The presence of woman is an indispensable element of spectacle in normal narrative film, yet her visual presence tends to work against the development of a story-line, to freeze the flow of action in moments of erotic contemplation' (Mulvey 1989: 19). In Cocteau's *La Belle et la Bête*, Beauty is precisely that, a passive, masochistic, object of beauty that attracts the active, sadistic male gaze. Josette Day acts the part of Beauty by taking up a series of statuesque poses (Figure 2.5), through which she demonstrates that she is aware of her status as object. Her every movement while in Beast's enchanted castle turns her into a '*tableau vivant*', adorned with jewels and rich clothing provided for her by him.

In *The Sadeian Woman and the Ideology of Pornography* feminist writer Angela Carter sums up women's roles, like that of Beauty, in traditional stories using a characteristically visceral metaphor. She says that women's 'symbolic value is primarily that of a myth of patience and receptivity, a dumb mouth from which the teeth have been pulled' (Carter 1993 [1979]: 4–5). Carter's own fantastic fairy tales, including those adapted for film by director Neil Jordan

Figure 2.5   'To-be-looked-at-ness' in *La Belle et la Bête*

in *The Company of Wolves* (1984), offer an alternative model of femininity and are concerned with, in Warner's words, a 'gallery of wonderful bad-good girls, beasts, rogues and other creatures' (1992: 25). Carter worked to deconstruct traditional fairy tales, for she says that 'all the mythic versions of women, from the myth of the redeeming purity of the virgin to that of the healing, reconciling mother, are consolatory nonsenses . . . to dull the pain of particular circumstances' (1993: 5).

These 'particular circumstances' are societal misogyny and oppression, and Aidan Day adds that Carter's subversive (re)telling of fairy tales 'was designed to help kill giants in the everyday, patriarchal world' (1998: 133). Warner writes of Carter's collection *The Old Wives' Fairy Tale Book* (1990) that she 'turns topsy-turvy some cautionary folk tales and shakes out the fear and dislike of women they once expressed to create a new set of values, about strong, outspoken, zestful, sexual women who can't be kept down' (in Carter 1990: x). In this way Carter gives women a different reflection to view in the identity-forming mirror stage, an alternative reflection in the magic mirror, which Haase describes as 'the metaphor that has dominated feminist investigations of the female subject in fairy tale texts' (2004: 23), and which Cristina Bacchilega sees as the 'controlling metaphor' of the fantasy tale (1997: 10).

FANTASY ADAPTATION

Feminist scholarship on fantasy helps bring to light not only some of the more conservative values that underpin fantasy storytelling, but also the many ways these often well-known stories get changed and adapted, updated and/or revised, to engage modern audiences. In the broadest sense, the adaptation of fantasy can be understood as an evolutionary process whereby a particular story in some form shifts, and an adaptation is likely to involve translation, transformation, (re)interpretation, (re)appropriation or (re)adjustment, for example from one culture to another, from one generation to another, or from one medium to another. As highlighted previously, this process of adaptation long predates the fantasy film and may be traced back to oral folk and fairy tale, legend and myth. Adaptation theorist Julie Sanders notes that these tradi-tional storytelling forms 'by their very nature depend on a communality of understanding . . . In this sense they participate in a very active way in a shared community of knowledge, and they have therefore proved particularly rich sources for adaptation and appropriation' (2006: 45). Indeed, we have already observed that fantasy films frequently either borrow from some aspects of myth, fairy tale or folklore as a basis for adaptation, or adopt them as a direct source.

Over time fantasy film has also developed strong ties with popular fantasy fiction like comics, pulp fiction and children's books. A brief look at the history of fantasy film demonstrates that many might be classified adaptations of one sort or another, from silent classics like *The Thief of Bagdad* (1924), to Hollywood films based on mythology, such as *Jason and the Argonauts* (1963) and *Clash of the Titans* (1981, remade in 2010), or Disney's (Americanized) animated film versions of (European) fairy tales, to the latest trend in blockbuster fantasy franchises adapted across a variety of media. For these reasons, and others we discuss, the concerns and questions raised by the process and theory of adaptation seem integral to the study of fantasy, as well as the enthusiasm for making and watching fantasy films.

In particular, debates about book to film adaptation have implications for a consideration of the creation and reception of fantasy on film. Typically at the forefront of such debates is the rather thorny issue of fidelity (see for example McFarlane 1996), and often the commercial and/or critical 'success' of a film adaptation has depended on whether the filmmakers can convince those viewers familiar with the adapted text that they have in some way remained faithful to the source novel or story. In creative terms, this calls attention to the many choices involved in the move from book to film, including the potential need to simplify, cut, update, emphasize, or even add or expand (especially if the source is a short story) some characters, sections or themes from the adapted text. Adaptation theorists now also stress the necessity to understand the meaning of these differences and the motivations behind them within the frame of specific social, historical, cultural and economic contexts (e.g. Hutcheon 2006).

Film technology is further recognized to play an important role in extending (or alternatively limiting) the possible creative options used by filmmakers when they transfer material from the page to the screen. One of the special challenges that the adaptation of some fantasy novels can present filmmakers is the need to translate the literary descriptions of fantastic transformations, characters and worlds imagined, into 'realistic' looking (if spectacular) visual images accompanied by sounds. There is a more detailed discussion of the impact of new technological breakthroughs on fantasy filmmaking in Chapter 3, but from the perspective of adaptation it is worth noting that the availability of new technologies such as CGI (computer-generated imagery), and the introduction of new kinds of filmmaking strategies, can result in adaptations of books which have not been filmed before, or which have perhaps been considered 'unfilmable' for years. In addition, these new technologies and strategies may result in remade film versions of previously adapted texts.

Media and critical responses to recent fantasy film adaptations like The Lord of the Rings and Harry Potter illustrate some of the above issues well and they have received much attention. In contrast to lesser-known fantasy works like Michael Ende's The Neverending Story, Frank Baum's The Wizard of Oz, or P.L. Travers's Mary Poppins children's books, which Deborah Cartmell says 'are normally overshadowed and/or overtaken by their film adaptation' (2007: 175), there is very little chance that any film version(s) of either The Lord of the Rings or Harry Potter could be thought capable of outstripping the much-loved novels they are based on. Tolkien and J.K. Rowling each had an established readership and a standing in popular culture which was vital for the filmmakers to take into account. Following the original publication of The Lord of the Rings in the mid-1950s, Tolkien's books achieved cult status as a classic work of twentieth-century fantasy fiction, and though there were adaptations made before Jackson's trilogy (including Ralph Bakshi's 1978 animated version and a BBC radio dramatization originally broadcast in 1981) the epic size and scope of the novels meant that many believed they would not transfer successfully to live-action film. Indeed, mainly because of the length and richness of detail, The Lord of the Rings books were widely thought to be unfilmable.

The Harry Potter novels also exemplify how fantasy literature might be problematic to adapt. When the first instalment of the film adaptation came out the novels themselves were still ongoing, they topped the bestsellers lists, and Harry Potter was already a popular phenomenon. Like Jackson and his team when they set about adapting The Lord of the Rings, the filmmakers starting production on *Harry Potter and the Philosopher's Stone* (2001) were naturally aware that the books had generated a following with expectations about the films. In each case the adapters were therefore faced with numerous important decisions to make (that viewers and critics would later examine and unpack), like what to leave in and what to take out, how best to solicit the target audience, and what the medium of film will (and will not) allow. Thanks to advancements in technology the story worlds of Harry Potter and Middle Earth are realized in imaginative ways that take advantage of the 'wonder' of the audiovisual techniques of contemporary film. This may in turn influence how fantasy novels are then (re-)read. For instance, Linda Hutcheon reflects that 'Now that I know what an enemy orc or a game of Quidditch (can) look like (from the movies), I suspect I will never be able to recapture my first imagined versions again' (2006: 29).

The *Harry Potter* and *The Lord of the Rings* film adaptations have each inevitably been considered in terms of the ongoing fidelity debate. In the case of the first Harry Potter film for example, Deborah Cartmell and Imelda Whelehan argue that 'a commitment to fidelity (in response to the perceived demands of readers/viewers) compromises the processes of adaptation' (2005: 37). We should perhaps add though that this nonetheless proved an exceptionally successful film at the box office, and in later instalments in the *Harry Potter* series other filmmakers have arguably been more interpretive about how they transfer the novels to the screen (see Nel 2009). There is also a great deal of interest in why, seemingly against the odds, so many people find *The Lord of the Rings* film adaptations effective. Much has been written about how faithful (or not) the film trilogy is to Tolkien's books, usually with reference to the changes made and the meanings of them. Jackson's decision not to include the character of Tom Bombadil in his film versions is widely noted, as are other choices made in the process of adaptation, such as the restructuring of the novels' story, and the greater emphasis on spectacular battle sequences like Helm's Deep. (For a more thorough comparison of *The Lord of the Rings* novels and films written by a Tolkien scholar, see Shippey 2004.)

Thomas Leitch reasons that the fairly 'free' approach Jackson took to the adaptation of *The Lord of the Rings* was 'More interested in fidelity to the larger design of Tolkien's epic than in fidelity to its component parts' (2007: 138).

This is possibly what makes audiences feel that Jackson successfully managed to capture what is commonly referred to as the 'spirit' of Tolkien's work, though according to Ian Hunter 'that spirit is often controversial and unhelpful' (2007: 158). In a study that discusses the problems of adapting a novel like The Lord of the Rings into a contemporary fantasy blockbuster, Hunter observes that 'some aspects of the story [such as the politics and view of women] might be hard to put over to a modern audience' (2007: 158). However, he also considers that other aspects of the books, like environmental issues, 'are drawn out in the films because of their contemporary resonance and applicability' and a few new elements introduced (Hunter 2007: 159). This is suggestive of the ways that fantasy adaptations can be understood as social, cultural, ideological and historical products, and also suggestive of the links between an adaptation and the reception context.

Christine Geraghty makes the valuable point about film adaptations that 'Faithfulness matters if it matters to the viewer' (2008: 3). In other words, and to apply this statement to fantasy adaptation, we might want to think about the differences between the viewing experiences of those unfamiliar with the original fantasy texts and those fans who know them very well, and all the various positions in between. For instance, what is the particular experience of someone who reads Harry Potter or The Lord of the Rings for the first time having watched the blockbuster fantasy adaptations? Lately, scholars have recognized the need to investigate more closely how actual audiences respond to adaptations and some research has shifted to include reception analysis. To date the largest attempt to study audience responses is The Lord of the Rings international audience research project, conducted by Martin Barker, Ernest Mathijs and others (2008). Contributors to this research use a wide range of materials, such as reviews, interviews, websites and audience questionnaires, to examine world responses to the final part of the film adaptation. The findings of this research are fascinating, and go some way to accomplishing the aims of the project, including questions of audience reception across national frames, and 'the functions and role of fantasy within contemporary culture' (Barker et al. 2008: 7).

Along with the consideration of aspects of audience response comes a discussion of the importance of fans. Of course, fantasy has tended to attract loyal fans who usually have very strong opinions about adaptations. In the age of the Internet, fan communities have become increasingly involved in adaptation, from the network of online sites that include forums which evaluate the film versions, to exchanges between filmmakers and fans. In the adaptation of *The Lord of the Rings* Jackson is generally thought to have balanced well the need to appeal to existing fans of the books with newcomers to the films. In particular, Jackson was strategic about the use of extended DVD versions of the films to reward the viewer with new footage, music and other extras. Such extended versions are part of a much wider intertext that includes the books, films, soundtracks, games, toys, and other consumer goods, interactions and experiences. As Hunter puts it, 'A film like *The Lord of the Rings* is a starting place as much as an end product of adaptation: just one reference point in a matrix of intertextual relations created by synergistic cross-promotion' (2007: 154).

These moves towards more intertextual views of adaptation are especially productive for the analysis of recent blockbuster fantasy film franchises. Robert Stam argues for a broad intertextual approach which is responsive to the many 'twists and turns' of adaptations (2005a: 5), rather than seeing them as a one- (or two-)way process. Comic book fantasy films, for example, often do not have a single or unchanging original/source text to adapt, and there are usually multiple different versions of a comic book hero across different decades and possibly media. (Two useful case studies include Will Brooker 1999, on Batman and adaptation, and Richard Berger 2008, on Superman and adaptation.) Elsewhere Stam comments that new media forms 'have already impacted upon adaptation and will do so even more in the future' (2005b: 12). Certainly, cross-media relations are heavily exploited by the most commercially successful fantasy franchises of the twenty-first century, from which a number of new areas for discussion emerge.

One of these areas increasingly explored is remediation, a term which Jay David Bolter and Richard Grusin (1999) use to describe the process that media use to 'refashion' one another. It is noted that in contemporary culture, fantasy films and video games are engaged in a process of mutual remediation, and there are significant crossover interactions between fantasy film and fantasy gaming. Just as popular fantasy films regularly get turned into games, so video games series, such as *Tomb Raider* and *Prince of Persia*, are sometimes made into Hollywood film adaptations. In *ScreenPlay: cinema/videogames/interfaces*, Geoff King and Tanya Krzywinska (2002) offer a collection of essays which examine interrelations between film and video games, approaching them as similar but distinct media forms and experiences. For King and Krzywinska, 'Forms such as games and cinema exist in complex and multidimensional relationships' (2002: 30), that can occur at various different levels, including genre, narrative and aesthetics. Fantasy-based Massively Multiplayer Online Role-Playing Games (MMORPGs) are also important, and Krzywinska suggests that a MMORPG like *World of Warcraft* remediates other mythic forms and sources to create a 'text richly populated with various allusions, correspondences and references' (2008: 123).

Another potential area of enquiry, and the last we propose in this chapter, is the emergence of transmedia fantasy. Transmedia is a term that describes the practice of content moving across closely integrated combinations of media. Transmediation may be considered a contemporary form of fantasy adaptation, where the makers of franchises such as *The Lord of The Rings* and *Harry Potter* routinely design, develop and release films, video games and other media simultaneously, building an enhanced story world which can be expanded and experienced in different ways by consuming each of them. In this respect Henry Jenkins's work on transmedia storytelling in the context of convergence culture is particularly insightful. 'More and more,' says Jenkins, 'storytelling has become the art of world building, as artists create compelling environments that cannot be fully explored or exhausted within a single work or even a single medium' (2006: 116). The phenomenon of transmedia fantasy franchises returns us to our initial discussion at the start of this section about new forms of storytelling and adaptations of fantasy. Many theorists compare the adaptation of stories to Darwinian evolution. In order for fantasy to survive and thrive in our contemporary culture surely we must hope that, however commercial this sometimes becomes, the process of transformation through adaptation is continued.

3

PRACTICAL MAGIC:
THE MAKING OF FANTASY FILM

In J.R.R. Tolkien's influential essay 'On Fairy-stories', he describes the importance of the self-coherent story world, which he calls the 'Secondary World', to the power and appeal of fantasy fiction for writers and readers. In a 'good' fantasy, he says:

> What really happens is that the story-maker proves a successful 'sub-creator'. He [*sic*] makes a Secondary World which your mind can enter. Inside it, what he [*sic*] relates is 'true': it accords with the laws of that world. You therefore believe it, while you are, as it were, inside. The moment disbelief arises, the spell is broken; the magic, or rather art, has failed. You are then out in the Primary World again.
>
> (Tolkien 1966: 60)

This is an observation that can also usefully be applied to the making of fantasy film, which is equally (if not even more) reliant on the ability of the 'sub-creator', in this case the filmmaker. Often it is the job of the fantasy filmmaker to cast a spell on the viewer by creating a consistent story world that is either separate from, or is in some way alternative to, our everyday reality. As we have discussed, this is an essential part of the magic of fantasy film.

In many cases the magic or art of the fantasy filmmaker, much like the fantasy writer, is then to make the unreal real, the impossible possible, and the unbelievable believable, in a logical and complete world that operates according to its own laws and functions within the parameters set by the story. So in the story worlds of some fantasy films, animals, birds, toys and even the odd teapot might talk and possibly also sing and dance, for example Disney's anthropomorphized animations. Though the story worlds of other fantasy films may look more like our own, they will usually differ from it in some important regard. For instance, *Practical Magic* (1998) the (admittedly rather forgettable) fantasy comedy drama that happens to share its name with the title of this chapter, is a story set in ordinary small-town America about love and female power, but with the additional elements of magic and witchcraft. It follows that, in the historical realms of fantasy filmmaking that concern us in this chapter, no two story makers, story worlds, or the spells they cast on audiences, are ever the same.

We might think of fantasy filmmaking as a form of practical magic. In general, the making of a film involves the practices of, among other things, screenwriting, directing, cinematography, sound, editing, lighting, acting, costume, makeup and set design, which occur at different stages in the production process. Together they create a familiar type of movie magic. In addition to these skills, the making of a fantasy film will typically require an extended list of specialist artists, teams of technicians, and whatever technological resources are available at the time of production. Invariably, fantasy is a demonstration of the practical magic of filmmaking at its most spectacular. Indeed, the quality and amount of expertise required to create the particular brand of practical magic needed for fantasy is routinely celebrated by the behind-the-scenes, making of, or special effects documentary 'exclusives' which accompany a film's release either at the cinema (when these documentaries are traditionally screened in advance on TV) or, more recently, on DVD. Starting with the first adaptation in the Harry Potter film series *Harry Potter and the Philosopher's Stone* (2001), the British television channel ITV screened one hour *Behind the Magic* specials in anticipation of the UK cinema release dates. Like the extras often found on special edition DVD versions of fantasy film (re-)releases old and new, these behind-the-scenes TV specials 'augment the film experience' (and potentially increase box-office takings) by producing an intertext that 'foregrounds the magic of Hollywood' (Klinger 2006b: 368), especially the technologies which impact on the use of special effects.

For writers and readers of literary fantasy the depiction of story worlds is usually restricted only by the possibilities of language or imagination. The makers and audiences of fantasy film however have also been affected by the possibilities and limitations of technology. For fantasy filmmakers, the ability to create a believable story world is often tied to new developments in cinema, particularly special effects technologies. In one of many DVD interviews, *The Lord of the Rings* trilogy (2001–2003) director Peter Jackson comments that the development of CGI finally made it possible for him to successfully adapt Tolkien's work into live-action films (cited in Friedman 2009). In fact, Ted Friedman (2009) suggests that, 'The 2000s have been a decade of fantasy [. . .] Now that Hollywood finally has the tools to do justice to the fantasy classics, it's making up for lost time'. Like other popular film genres, such as science fiction and horror, which need to make the imaginary appear convincingly real, the evolution of fantasy film is clearly dependent on the development of technology. It is also important to consider that a significant number of technological advances throughout the history of cinema have been pioneered by the makers of fantasy films, from technical innovations in early cinema to the digital effects used in contemporary blockbusters.

To some extent, this account of some of the key developments in the history of fantasy film is linked to what is for most of us by now a familiar critical debate about 'spectacle versus narrative' in cinema. This is because, once again, along with other spectacle-based film genres like horror and science fiction, the use of effects sequences in fantasy films has been said to disrupt the progression of narrative. Stephen Keane gives a helpful summary of the basic tension that lies behind this argument:

> Whereas narrative is classically said to give drive, coherence and meaning to a film, spectacle has traditionally been regarded in terms of self-contained moments of visual excess. Seen in these terms, spectacle in effect short-circuits narrative, almost putting the film on hold while we're

pulled into some other dimension where action and effects take over from 'natural' storytelling properties and dramatic revelations.

(2007: 57)

The recent growth in CGI-dominated fantasy films has undoubtedly done much to fuel these debates about the relationship between spectacle and storytelling in contemporary cinema (see King 2000). However, as Keane also points out, this criticism is actually far from new (2007: 57) and, to start with, we will locate its origins in the fantasy films of Georges Méliès and what Tom Gunning (1990) has described as the early 'cinema of attractions'. As such, this chapter will go on to identify some of the ways in which narrative and spectacle are often related in fantasy story worlds.

Returning to the words of Tolkien that open this chapter, there is one further note to make about our approach to the history of fantasy film. According to Tolkien, one of the main attractions that the story world of fantasy holds for the audience is an imaginative escape from the primary or known world and real life. However it is important to remember that this does not mean that fantasy story worlds are unable or unwilling to engage with the primary real worlds in which they are produced and consumed. Rather, as we have argued, fantasy is about much more than escapism and, typical of cinema, there is often a direct correlation between the making of fantasy films and major social, cultural and ideological shifts.

The following historical overviews in this chapter focus variously on key production and technological factors that shape the magic and evolution of fantasy on screen, on the significance of the social events and cultural backdrops against which some of these films were originally made, and on the audiences who watch them. We concentrate mainly on live-action fantasy; though the development of animation and its impact on fantasy in film, especially when it is used in combination with live-action, does not go unacknowledged (see Wells 1998, 2002 for detailed discussions of animation). This chapter is divided into two sections. The first section takes a broadly chronological approach and examines some of the most important influences on fantasy film. In the second section we move on to look at some specific technological innovations and how they relate to fantasy. Rather than give a comprehensive list, this chapter asks the reader to think critically about the making of fantasy films in selected historical, industrial and technological contexts.

INDUSTRY AND AUDIENCES

Even before cinema was established as a popular form of entertainment, Victorian exhibitors used a combination of magic tricks and technological spectacles to attract audiences. Film historians have discussed how early cinema emerged from nineteenth-century exhibition cultures that included vaudeville magic shows and demonstrations of optical and scientific technologies (see Popple and Kember 2004). Pre-cinema optical entertainments, such as shadow plays, phantasmagoria and magic lantern shows, were particularly influential on the association between early film and fantasy. Some magic lantern shows are said to have projected painted slides that drew on fairy stories and contained fantastic figures such as imps, skeletons or an Aladdin's lamp complete with genie. These slides could be passed slowly in front of the lens in order to tell a story and exhibitors sometimes attempted early uses of special effects whereby, for instance, the head of a skeleton appeared to float over the audience (Warner 2006: 155).

Fantasy in early film

In most accounts of film history, French filmmaker Méliès is credited as the founding father of cinematic fantasy and a pioneer of special effects. Before moving into filmmaking, Méliès was a professional magician and many of the theatrical tricks he performed were later incorporated into what were labelled his 'trick' films. In his short trick films Méliès regularly used stop-motion substitution, multiple exposures and dissolves to recreate familiar illusions for the camera. In the three-minute-long 1902 trick film L'Homme à la Tête de Caoutchouc/The Man with the Rubber Head for example, a scientist played by Méliès inflates a duplicate of his own head to a gigantic size (Figure 3.1) and then releases air to contract it again. When his assistant has a go, much to the scientist's dismay, he over-inflates the head and it finally explodes in a cloud of smoke to comic effect.

Figure 3.1   Georges Méliès appears to inflate a double of his head in *L'Homme à la Tête de Caoutchouc*

The illusion of the head inflating in *L'Homme á la Tête de Caoutchouc* was achieved using a series of superimpositions: the background remains static throughout, but the superimposed copy of Méliès's head was filmed with a camera that moved towards and away from it, which creates the illusion of expansion and contraction. Other trick films made by Méliès feature dismemberment (e.g. *Un Homme de Têtes/The Four Troublesome Heads*, 1898), replication (e.g. *L'Homme Orchestre/One Man Band*, 1900), the transformation of a woman into her likeness in *Le Portrait Spirituel/The Spiritualist Photographer* (1903), and a man who appears to walk up walls and on the ceiling in *L'Homme Mouche/The Human Fly* (1902). These early uses of cinematic illusions and in-camera effects gave Méliès the ability to seemingly manipulate and transform what the viewer sees. The metamorphosis effects that he initiated became central to the visual aesthetics of fantasy and no doubt inspired many future developments in film technology such as CGI (Ndalianis 2000: 261). As a filmmaker, Méliès experimented with technically imaginative ways of exploiting the cinematic medium to bring a new kind of magic to the screen.

In addition to trick films, David Robinson identifies the féeries or fantasy films as 'perhaps Méliès' most characteristic work' (1993: 35). These are heavily theatrical films which often contain fairy tale motifs, settings and characters and use many of the same techniques to create spectacle. Méliès's major féeries include Cendrillon/Cinderella (1899), Le Petite Chaperon Rouge/Little Red Riding Hood (1901), Les Hallucinations du Baron de Munchausen/Baron Munchausen's Dream (1911), and the most widely recognized of his works (also considered the first science fiction film), Le Voyage dans le Lune/A Trip to the Moon (1902). His 1899 Cendrillon is a multiple-shot story that, unlike his short and effects-driven trick films, combines a longer narrative with spectacular elements to adapt Charles Perrault's version of the classic fairy tale. The use of dissolves in this film allows a series of tableau scenes to link together in a pattern of cause and effect, and stop-motion substitutions make it possible for mice to magically grow into footmen and a pumpkin to change into a coach.

Méliès is particularly renowned for his early use of an elaborate mise-en-scène to help tell the story and create depth and atmosphere. He had a glass studio constructed in Paris so that he could film indoors: the studio contained a stage that, when equipped with trap doors, trick panels and flying rigs, was especially suited to the filming of fantasy sequences and effects. Using costumes, props and painted scenery, tableaux scenes were staged in this indoor setting for a stationary camera in what has been compared to a theatrical-style presentation (Kracauer 1997 [1960]: 33). This is evident in Cendrillon: painted backdrops recreate the fairy tale's original settings, including the Prince's palace ballroom and the villa owned by Cinderella's father; the film's wealthy characters wear lavish costumes which help to establish the mood of this romantic fantasy, and props like clocks are used to create drama by reminding the viewer of the time when the fairy godmother's magical spell will be broken. Méliès also had some frames in his films hand-tinted. When the fairy godmother makes her first appearance in Cendrillon for instance, she wears a magenta dress and an amber crown. In this way, besides the novelty value of watching these moving pictures, Méliès's fantasy films entertained early audiences with the use of visual effects and a distinctive style and mise-en-scène.

Of course, though highly influential, Méliès was certainly not the only filmmaker in the early history of film with the ability to create notable fictional worlds. In Britain, Robert W. Paul collaborated with Walter R. Booth on films using trick effects, including the early sword and sorcery romance *The Magic Sword* (1901), and Cecil B. Hepworth and Percy Stow made the first screen version of Lewis Carroll's *Alice in Wonderland* in 1903. In the US, Edwin S. Porter experimented with animation in *The Dream of a Rarebit Fiend* (1906). Another Frenchman, Ferdinand Zecca, produced short films for Pathé studios which also often used fantasy, such as *Ali Baba et les Quarante Voleurs/Ali Baba and the Forty Thieves* (1902) (see Christie 1994: 7–37).

In Chapter 2, we examined critical debates about the fantasy/realism divide in cinema. This began with the supposed dichotomy between on the one hand, the Lumière-style non-fiction *actualité* films and, on the other hand, the use of *mise-en-scène* and innovations in effects in order to explore cinema's fantastic potential, most often associated with the trick and fantasy films of Méliès. In both cases, the cinema (technology and the illusion of movement) itself is understood as a source of spectacle for early film audiences. As a result, Gunning has called early cinema (pre-1906/7) a 'cinema of attractions', in which the film 'directly solicits spectator attention, inciting visual curiosity, and supplying pleasure through an exciting spectacle – a unique event . . . that is of interest in itself' (1990: 58). Gunning argues that, for early narrative filmmakers like Méliès, storytelling was a pretext for linking together a series of attractions motivated by the display of spectacle.

This emphasis on spectacle in 'primitive' cinema changed with the emergence of conventional narrative storytelling (post-1907), and also with the development of what became known as classical Hollywood cinema (1917–1960, according to Bordwell, Staiger and Thompson 1985). Nevertheless, it is widely acknowledged that the 'cinema of attractions' has not disappeared. Gunning suggests that in the 1980s spectacular filmmaking 'reaffirmed its roots . . . in what might be called the Spielberg–Lucas–Coppola cinema of effects' (1990: 67). We will see that the extent to which some contemporary Hollywood franchises might 'show' audiences rather than 'tell' them further reinforces the suggestion that the 'cinema of attractions' still persists today, especially in blockbuster fantasy film.

Fantasy and the European avant-garde

Avant-garde and experimental film is also influential to the ongoing evolution of fantasy on screen. Much like early cinema, European-centred art movements such as surrealism and expressionism sit outside the development of commercial studio production and therefore they also sit outside mainstream genre conventions, like those of fantasy film (Sobchack 1996: 313). Even so, not only do the ideas of fantasy and imagination have very strong links with both the surrealist and expressionist movements, but the style and techniques used by these avant-garde film artists have been taken up by some later American and European fantasy filmmakers.

Surrealism began as a revolutionary cultural movement (including artists, writers and filmmakers) in 1920s France that grew out of the activities of Dada, a group of artists opposed to the First World War. The surrealists, like the Dada artists before them, shared a political opposition to the dominant culture of the time; they used incongruous juxtapositions and fantastic imagery to express the workings of the unconscious mind and to question social taboos. The dreamlike quality of film made it an ideal medium for the surrealists to explore associations, gaps, chance, slips, fantasies and desires in ways that challenge conventional linear notions of narrative, character development, and cause and effect storytelling. Susan Hayward summarizes that: 'Surrealist films are concerned with . . . the liberating force of unconscious desires and fantasy that are normally repressed' (2000: 378).

In early surrealist films, such as Spanish filmmaker Luis Buñuel and artist Salvador Dalí's *Un Chien Andalou / An Andalusian Dog* (1928) and *L'âge D'or / The Golden Age* (1930), it is the imagery and logic of dreams that is followed, rather than the codes and continuity of narrative cinema. *Un Chien Andalou* uses discontinuous editing to fragment both time and space. Sequences of graphic matches play on the similarities between various shapes and patterns, such as a hand crawling with ants, followed by a hairy armpit, followed by a sea urchin. The use of these techniques means that, in the opinion of the surrealists, the viewer is left free to make associations which are not based on character psychology or a causal narrative, and disorientation allows the mind to create new (and unconscious) meanings. That the images used in the surrealist films are often sexual, violent, bizarre and/or darkly humorous – the eyeball slicing scene and the two dead donkeys on grand pianos (Figure 3.2) in *Un Chien Andalou* are very well known examples – suggests the disturbing potential of fantasy and dreams and hints at Freudian theories on the function of the unconscious. Another filmmaker often mentioned in association with European surrealism is French poet and artist Jean Cocteau. Cocteau adapted fairy tales and Greek myth in avant-garde films like *La Belle et la Bête/Beauty and the Beast* (1946) and *Orphée/Orpheus* (1950) to create surrealist fantasy worlds filled with strange imagery, such as candelabras held by disembodied human arms, and where mirrors are gateways.

Surrealism has also been present in Eastern Europe, and has proven especially influential in Czech film culture (Richardson 2006: 121). The works of Czech surrealist artist Jan Švankmajer, including short and feature films, are widely regarded as important examples of international fantasy filmmaking that have gained a cult following. Švankmajer's films use a combination of puppetry, animation and live-action and often refer to the fantasy worlds of folk and fairy tales, myths, and magic. *Poslední trik pana Schwarcewalldea a pana Edgara/The Last Trick* (1964) is a short film by Švankmajer about two conjurers who seek to outdo one another. In another of his shorts, *Zvahlav aneb Saticky Slameného Huberta/Jabberwocky* (1971), a reading of Carroll's poem is accompanied by disturbing imagery like dead animals and dismembered dolls.

Figure 3.2
Surreal imagery in
Un Chien Andalou

Neco z Alenky/Alice (1988) is Švankmajer's first feature film and is a subversive retelling of Carroll's story which explores the dark psychological and sexual undercurrents of Wonderland from the perspective of a child, and *Lekce Faust/Faust* (1994) is an experimental interpretation of the myth of Dr Faustus. Taken in the context of the former Czechoslovakia, it is significant that, like his French and Spanish counterparts, Švankmajer's surrealist films can be understood as part of a subversive cinema pessimistic about capitalism and the totalitarian state (Coombs 2007: 10–11). Švankmajer has continued to make surrealist fantasy films in what is now the Czech Republic. For example, made in 2000 *Otesánek/Little Otik* is a striking surreal comic version of a Czech folktale about a childless couple who adopt a tree stump that looks like a baby.

Outside the tradition of surrealism in European art cinema, more mainstream filmmakers use some surrealist imagery and the iconography and syntax of dreaming to explore notions of fantasy. Directors like Alfred Hitchcock, David Lynch, Spike Jonze and David Cronenberg have made films that rely heavily on dreamlike juxtapositions, fragmented narratives, and Freudian symbolism to confuse and challenge audiences. In Lynch's *Eraserhead* (1977) and *Mulholland Drive* (2001), labyrinthine narratives and surreal dream imagery act as puzzles for the audience to interpret or 'solve'. Though such films are not surrealist in the sense that either Buñuel or Švankmajer's works are, they do contain moments of surrealism, or elements of a surrealist style, that engage with the surrealist fascination with desire, drives, the dream and death, and these remain a vital part of the 'dark side' (Creed 2007: 113–18) of fantasy in cinema.

The style and aesthetic of German expressionism also lends itself to the darker side of fantasy in film. German expressionism (arguably part of a wider expressionist avant-garde art movement) emerged in post-First World War Weimer Germany and thrived during the early 1920s when the films met with international success. The expressionist films use chiaroscuro lighting, highly stylized sets and tilted/canted frames and angles to create an exaggerated and abstract *mise-en-scène* that uses these visual codes for a disturbed emotional and psychological narrative. Quintessential German expressionist films such as Robert Wiene's *Das Cabinet des Dr Caligari/The Cabinet of Dr Caligari* (1920) and Frederick W. Murnau's *Nosferatu* (1922) are set in distorted and macabre artificial worlds and contain fantastic characters which later inspired horror cinema. The influence of these expressionist films on the development of the horror genre is well documented and, as Brigid Cherry observes, 'many accounts of horror begin with these films' (2009: 65).

Appropriately though, Thomas Elsaesser (1996) views German expressionism not so much as a new departure in the country's output, but as part of a dominant tradition in German national cinema: the fantastic film. In particular, Elsaesser looks back to the pre-war films that Paul Wegener acted in (e.g. *Der Rattenfänger von Hameln/The Pied Piper of Hamelin*, 1918), which he says exploited established national literary trends for fairy and folk stories and 'created the genre of the Gothic-Romantic fairy tale film' (1996: 141). This argument is important because it reminds us that most, if not all, nations have their own traditions of fantasy and storytelling which often predate cinema and which continue to influence styles and modes of fantasy filmmaking.

Like the earlier fantastic films of German cinema, a number of expressionist films, such as Fritz Lang's *Der Müd Tod/Destiny* (1921), his two-part version of the national epic *Die Nibelungen/The Nibelungen* (1924), and Murnau's *Faust* (1926), explored popular fairy tales and myths. Expressionism functioned to create stylized settings for fantasy stories. As a result, David Bordwell and Kristin Thompson state that 'Expressionist films depended greatly on their designers' (2004: 473), and in the German studios like UFA (where Lang and Murnau were based) such film technicians were often well paid and had high professional reputations. *Die Nibelungen* was filmed on studio sets (featuring medieval castles and misty forests) designed and constructed by Otto Hunte, Erich Kettlehut and Karl Vollbrecht to create a large-scale story world. Expressionist devices were used by Lang (and cinematographer Walter Ruttmann) to layer symbolism and visualize dream images, such as the animated 'dream of the falcon' sequence in *Part 1: Siegfried*, where two stylized black eagles attack a white falcon, which acts as a portent of Siegfried's death. The film is also notable for its groundbreaking use of special effects, including a 50-foot mechanical dragon. The German expressionist movement came to an end by 1927, and Lang left Germany and moved to the US at the beginning of the Nazi regime in 1933. Nevertheless, *Die Nibelungen*'s nationalistic fantasy attracted attention from the party leaders and fantasy film became part of Nazi-era cinema (e.g. *Münchhausen*, 1943).

In addition to the direct influence of filmmakers like Lang who moved from Germany to the US film industry during the 1930s, from this time onwards many of the stylized techniques used by the expressionists were incorporated into Hollywood cinema. Beyond the horror genre, where the impact of expressionism is quite obvious, its effects can further be seen across a wide range of film types and styles from film noir in the 1940s and 1950s, to Hitchcock, to more recent science fiction cinema like *Blade Runner* (1982) and *Dark City* (1998), and the fantasy films of Terry Gilliam and Tim Burton. In films such as *Batman/Batman Returns* (1989/1992), *Edward Scissorhands* (1990) and *Charlie and the Chocolate Factory* (2005), Burton uses German expressionist-inspired *mise-en-scène* and set design to create modern gothic fairy tale worlds and characters that often play with the boundaries between inner and outer light and darkness.

Fantasy filmmaking in the Hollywood studio era

The Hollywood tradition of fantasy filmmaking, which tells stories via classical narrative and special effects, developed under the studio system. From the 1930s to the 1940s the Hollywood studios possessed an unrivalled ability to make, distribute and exhibit films to domestic and international audiences. Since the economic and industrial structures of this enormously successful system have already been surveyed extensively elsewhere (see Bordwell *et al.* 1985; Maltby 2003), in this overview we focus our attention on some of the ways fantasy was taken up in the studio era.

One result of the organization of the studio system was that each major studio established an in-house special effects department and effects were increasingly important to the economy and style of many films made in Hollywood. During the early silent era, as for example in Méliès's fantasy films, most 'trick' effects were created in the camera itself (usually by the cinematographer or camera assistants), using skilled and time-consuming procedures. By the studio era, however, effects work became increasingly specialized and the studios required film technicians with specific areas of expertise. Now familiar special effects techniques that played a key role during the studio era include rear projection, travelling mattes, and optical printing. Not only could these special effects be used to save production companies a lot of time and money (especially when the coming of sound in the early 1930s made it necessary to film mainly in the controlled conditions of an indoor studio set), when needed they also supplied spectacle and fantasy (Balio 1995: 131–5).

The RKO fantasy film *King Kong* (1933) is commonly cited as an example of the technical achievements made in special effects during the studio system. Mostly shot in the studio, *King Kong* required numerous effects techniques, including stop-motion animation, matting, miniature rear projection and optical work. For instance, the climactic scene where Kong climbs the Empire State Building uses a combination of effects, described by Kenneth Von Gunden (1989: 103–19) in his account of the film's production process: frame-by-frame stop-motion animation makes an 18-inch model Kong appear to ascend a miniature of the New York skyscraper; close-ups of full-scale models of his head and hand are integrated to make it look like he is holding actress Fay Wray; and shots of real biplanes are intercut with models so that Kong seems to realistically interact with them (Figure 3.3). Characteristic of studio system production methods, *King Kong* was also worked on by regular RKO contract personnel such as co-director/producer Merian C. Cooper, music composer Max Steiner, and art director Carroll Clark.

Figure 3.3
Special effects:
Kong on top of
the Empire State
Building, where
he is attacked
by biplanes in
the finale of
King Kong

Despite notable successes like *King Kong*, fantasy was, as Bordwell remarks, a 'minor genre of the studio years', later boosted by the triumph of George Lucas's New Hollywood blockbuster *Star Wars* in 1977 (2006: 53). In contrast to some film genres, like horror and the musical, which became associated with specific studios (Universal and MGM respectively), no one Hollywood studio can really be said to dominate live-action fantasy filmmaking during the classical period, though films with some element of fantasy were released by most of the motion picture companies. More often, the talents of individual technicians and sometimes special effects departments are recognized to have shaped aspects of the fantasy film in this era. In the case of *King Kong*, it was special effects coordinator Willis O'Brien who, having revolutionized stop-motion photography in the animation of dinosaurs in the *The Lost World* (1925), is understood to have created the film's distinctive look and made Kong an emotive and lifelike fantasy creature.

Other live-action films with strong elements of fantasy made by Hollywood studios at the height of the classical era include: from MGM *Topper* (1937), *The Wizard of Oz* (1939) and *Cabin in the Sky* (1943); from RKO *The Devil and Daniel Webster/All That Money Can Buy* (1941) and *It's a Wonderful Life* (1947), and from Columbia *Lost Horizon* (1937) and *Here Comes Mr Jordan* (1941). In these films fantasy is combined with other genres to produce fantasy mixes, like fantasy musicals, fantasy adventures, fantasy comedies and fantasy romances, all of which still remain important to Hollywood and popular today. *The Wizard of Oz*, in particular, was one of MGM's most expensive films of the 1930s and used an all-star cast (including long-term contract star Judy Garland in the lead role of Dorothy Gale), lavish studio sets and spectacular effects techniques to create a musical fantasy. Even though the enormous costs meant that *The Wizard of Oz* lost money on its first run in 1939, the film made a large profit in later years and has since been regarded as an American fantasy classic, where it consistently ranks highly in annual 'Greatest Films' lists. Though fantasy was not a dominant presence in the studio era we must not overlook the use of fantasy in some big budget films made by the studios, nor should we forget that many have had an enduring appeal to audiences.

In the 1930s and 1940s the Great Depression and the Second World War are thought to have impacted on the film industry both commercially and artistically; not only did an economic downturn and wartime affect the 'business' of Hollywood, these conditions also affected the style and subjects of its entertainment. Many studies of Depression era and wartime Hollywood suggest that, for better or worse, the majority of films made in this period were escapist. For the price of a cinema ticket, audiences in America and Europe could temporarily escape the realities of economic or wartime deprivation, damage and distress and spend two hours elsewhere, if not in an out-and-out fantasy world then at least in a fantasy placed somewhere else which usually ended happily ever after. On one level this was, and often still is, true, as very few Hollywood films can really be said to depict contemporary social conditions in a hard-hitting or realistic way. But as we already know, it is rare that such films (or filmmakers), fantasy included, do not in some way allude to real world conditions, such as economic depression and war, and escapism is usually only part of a larger picture.

To illustrate we return to the film adaptation of *The Wizard of Oz* which uses the Depression and the hard social and economic conditions of the 1930s Dust Bowl as the backdrop to a fantasy story about a little girl longing to escape. As a result, some readings of the film stress the ideologically conservative message behind Dorothy's circular journey from Kansas to Oz and back again, and the fantasy solution 'there's no place like home'. Audiences at the time of the film's release would likely associate this phrase with the many American farmers who were dispossessed or struggling to make a living. To those suffering during America's Depression, these words and the lesson Dorothy learns, 'If I ever go looking for my heart's desire again, I won't look any further than my own backyard', might in actual fact reassure them not to flee and to struggle on through the hard times. It is interesting that for viewers today, Dorothy's famous chant as she clicks her heels towards the film's end can serve as a nostalgic reminder of the importance of the place or person that we each call home and the values and comfort this represents. In this way her words also carry with them a universal message that travels across social, cultural and historical boundaries and helps to afford this Depression era fantasy film 'widespread popularity and staying power' (Mackey-Kallis 2001: 126).

A group of Hollywood films released during and just after the Second World War likewise tapped into fantasy in culturally significant ways.

Supernatural films such as *A Guy Named Joe* (1944), *The Enchanted Cottage* (1945) and *The Ghost and Mrs Muir* (1947) used fantasy as a way to deal with disfigurement, death and the loss of a loved one at a time when this was a widespread reality. In *A Guy Named Joe* a dead pilot, Pete, is assigned to a heavenly air force division and sent back down to earth to train a new young pilot, Ted. The story of Ted's transformation into a hero is tied to a romantic plotline in which both Pete and his grieving girlfriend Dorinda must learn to accept his death (this happens as she gradually falls in love with Ted). Typically in this sort of story the happy ending is brought about thanks to divine or supernatural intervention. In contrast to supernatural occurrences in the horror genre though (which are invariably designed to frighten the viewer), the ghosts, hauntings and mysterious events in this cycle of fantasy films are rarely anything other than friendly and/or helpful and act to reaffirm the strength and power of romantic love. Peter Valenti argues that these films were more than escapist fantasies about 'death transcended . . . and the shaping influences of cosmic spiritual powers over the mortal world' (2003: 97). In the war and post-war years he says that they also provided a patriotic message and positive 'cultural sustenance' (Valenti 2003: 103) to audiences weary of the war effort and its toll on human life. Elsewhere, Valenti (1978: 294–304) suggests the term 'film blanc' in an attempt to describe a variety of feel-good wartime fantasy films which, in contrast to film noir, offer optimism and reassurance.

Like *The Wizard of Oz*, Frank Capra's post-war film *It's a Wonderful Life* has captivated audiences and is now considered another classic fantasy of the studio era. The film stars James Stewart as George Bailey, a man who is in crisis because he feels his life is worthless. When George contemplates suicide on the town bridge he is confronted by a fledgling angel who shows him a dystopian fantasy world of what life would be like for others in his small community had he not been born. That George is responding to disappointments such as his inability to enlist in the war (due to an injury he suffered during childhood when he saved his brother), and also to the threat of bankruptcy of his father's Building and Loan company which he has fought hard to save, is yet another example of how fantasy is used as a means to address some of the real world social problems experienced by film audiences at the time. However, in the context of the studio system this practice has tended to be viewed as sentimental or cynical (or even cynically sentimental) in support of the dominant Hollywood ideology and economy.

For example, in a review for the *New York Times*, Bosley Crowther complimented some of the characters, the acting and the drama in *It's a Wonderful Life*, but ultimately concluded that:

> the weakness of this picture, from this reviewer's point of view, is the sentimentality of it – its illusory concept of life. Mr Capra's nice people are charming, his small town is a quite beguiling place and his pattern for solving problems is most optimistic and facile. But somehow they all resemble theatrical attitudes rather than average realities.
>
> (1946: 19)

Crowther emphasized the heavily theatrical style with which this 'moralistic fable' (1946: 19) was delivered by Capra, and watching *It's a Wonderful Life* was considered by him to be an emotional but unsatisfying 'illusory' experience for the viewer. Indeed, the powers of such recuperative happy endings in fantasy are often problematized by film scholars. Robin Wood (2004) notes that though the audience sees George safely returned to his 'real' hometown and family in Bedford Falls, the villain Mr Potter goes unpunished for stealing the money that almost bankrupted George's firm and drove him to the brink of suicide. For Wood, 'The film recognizes explicitly that behind every Bedford Falls lurks a Pottersville' (2004: 723), a place that is outwardly noir-ish with its dark and moody *mise-en-scène*. This refusal to either redeem or remove Potter from Bedford Falls effectively serves to limit the external optimism at the film's conclusion, and a believable happy ending is not reached because the same underlying tensions still exist.

These days, historical distance has, as Jonathan Munby (2000) comments in a collection of essays on the Christmas film, largely detached *It's a Wonderful Life* from the lived experiences of the Depression and war that 'haunted' its original reception. Due to annual screenings on television (from the mid-1970s onwards) and the nostalgic 'mythification' of the 1930s and 1940s, he says that *It's a Wonderful Life* has become 'the Christmas movie' (Munby 2000:

54–5, emphasis in original), and a standard by which other Hollywood Christmas films are judged. Munby observes that for more recent audiences, It's a Wonderful Life 'assumes an ahistorical immanent status – and the darker (demystifying or sobering) elements of the film lose their power to interfere with the affirmative story and its fantasy of a happy end' (2000: 55). In other words, the film has become a heart-warming seasonal reminder of how each one of us has something to contribute to our community and a universal message of hope, which most of us will watch on television at least once. This shift in interpretation is particularly significant as it demonstrates the importance of paying attention to the changing social and cultural contexts in which fantasy films are made and received.

It's a Wonderful Life was released towards the end of what many film historians call the 'golden age' years of classic Hollywood (see Schatz 1999). Though the decline of the studio system obviously did not stop the involvement of the Hollywood majors in fantastic films in the 1950s and 1960s, it altered what they produced and how they appealed to audiences at a time when cinema attendance generally dropped. (We discuss later on in this chapter that by the early 1960s more technological innovations took hold, aimed at competing with TV.) For instance, a cycle of giant monster movies including The Beast From 2,000 Fathoms (1953) and It Came From Beneath the Sea (1955) were marketed to the new youth audience in the 1950s. Such fantastic films were mostly low budget (and often referred to as 'B-movies') but usually also vehicles for large-scale visual effects. Stop-motion expert Ray Harryhausen famously produced spectacular animated creatures for many of these films, and The 7th Voyage of Sinbad (1958) was the first in a series of fantasy films he made based on the Arabian Nights tales and Greek myths (e.g. Jason and the Argonauts, 1963).

In contrast to the fantastic films made to attract young audiences, some studios concentrated on fewer but more expensive 'A' productions targeted mainly at a traditional family audience. Disney was already closely associated with popular family and fantasy films. In the 1960s the company achieved box-office success with animated features like The Sword in the Stone (1963) and The Jungle Book (1967), and also moved more into live-action films such as The Absent Minded Professor (1961) and Mary Poppins (1964). The musical fantasy

Mary Poppins cost Disney $5.2 million to make (Balio 1987: 127) and combined live-action, special effects and animation to create magical sequences where an untidy room is cleaned up at a snap of the fingers, and the characters enter a pavement chalk drawing into an animated world where they sing and dance with penguin waiters. Peter Krämer points out that, in this transitional period in Hollywood history, *Mary Poppins* was widely publicized and pre-sold based on a fantasy story (by P.L. Travers), had a bestselling soundtrack, a big budget and went to great lengths to offer cinema audiences 'an overwhelming, in many ways unique experience' (2005: 28). This made *Mary Poppins* a 'calculated [fantasy] blockbuster' (Krämer 2005: 28–9) in some ways comparable to the hits of contemporary Hollywood which come next.

Contemporary Hollywood and the fantasy blockbuster franchise

In critical accounts of the Hollywood blockbuster, 'Lucas-Spielberg syndrome' (Wood 1986: 165) and the box-office success of *Star Wars*, *Raiders of the Lost Ark* (1981) and *E.T.: The Extra-Terrestrial* (1982) are heralded as beginning new trends in filmmaking which had long-lasting effects on the film industry. In such accounts, Lucas and Steven Spielberg are usually credited with (or alternatively held responsible for) having revitalized Hollywood and made big budget visually spectacular fantasy films very popular. Lucas and Spielberg dominated many aspects of mainstream genre filmmaking (including what audiences expected), and the blockbusters they made from the late 1970s onwards became the model for the many fantasy franchises launched by Hollywood today.

Star Wars's now legendary status as the film that began a global phenomenon makes it an obvious fantasy blockbuster to start this discussion of contemporary Hollywood cinema. It must be acknowledged that to claim *Star Wars* is a fantasy is not entirely straightforward. The film's setting in space, iconography of spaceships, robots and lightsabers and cast of alien creatures mean that it is often placed in the science fiction genre. Many critics, however, take note of *Star Wars*'s broader generic references. J.P. Telotte observes that *Star Wars* is 'in effect a homage to a great number of films and film types –

the western, war films, Japanese Samurai films – all of which have contributed to Lucas' vision here, as well as to the collective cinematic unconscious of his intended audience' (2001: 105). And in his study of film genre, Barry Langford (2005) points out *Star Wars*'s debt to classic swashbucklers, such as *The Black Pirate* (1926) and *The Adventures of Robin Hood* (1938). This link is apparent when 'Luke vaults across the fathomless core unit in the Death Star clasping Princess Leia in his arms' (Langford 2005: 238). These are to name just a few of the many films and genres referenced by *Star Wars*'s pastiche, and in an interview Lucas himself stated 'Do not call this film science fiction, it's a space fantasy' (in Pye and Miles 1999: 81). This classification seems particularly apt if we recall the film's traditional fairy tale-style opening 'A long time ago, in a galaxy far, far away . . .', its mythical quest narrative, and the magical power of the Force which Luke must learn to master.

The preference expressed by Lucas for the label of space fantasy rather than science fiction is suggestive of a hybrid approach to film genre. Spielberg's early work reveals a similarly wide range of inspirations and E.T., for example, combines the characteristics of science fiction with a plot that is more closely associated with fairy tale fantasy, and includes elements of comedy and family melodrama. Andrew Gordon (2008) reads E.T. as an updated version of the Brothers Grimm fairy tale 'The Frog-King', a story of magic and transformation. He then compares the sentimental ending of E.T. to that of the classical Hollywood fantasy musical *The Wizard of Oz*, because he says that both show the audience the 'journey we all must take to return to the place at our heart's core: "Home"' (Gordon 2008: 90).

We have already noted how fantasy films made during the studio era were often cross-generic, for instance mixing fantasy with the musical and/or comedy. Genre hybridity is, therefore, certainly not new to the contemporary era (see Staiger 2003), but with the blockbuster has come a heightened self-consciousness manifested in the multi-genre film productions that emerged with *Star Wars*, and continue in other Hollywood fantasy. Jackson's *The Lord of the Rings* trilogy is a case in point. Generally speaking the trilogy is considered fantasy, but as Kristin Thompson highlights, 'it mixes conventions of several popular genres into its overarching fantasy structure: martial arts action, horror, swashbucklers, war and even hints of Westerns' (2008b: 57). It is this genre mixing, she argues, that 'helped make it into such a broad success', by appealing to audiences beyond those who might read Tolkien or those who normally watch fantasy films (Thompson 2008b: 57).

Though high concept films like *Star Wars*, *Raiders of the Lost Ark* and *E.T.* played well to cinema audiences, the blockbuster mentality that took hold in Hollywood fantasy attracted much criticism. Many film scholars argue that during the late 1970s and into the 1980s (and beyond) Hollywood cinema was certainly populist but also overwhelmingly juvenile, nostalgic, and reactionary. Wood originally used the term 'Lucas-Spielberg syndrome', cited at the beginning of this overview, to critique simplistic blockbuster 'films catering to the desire for regression to infantilism, the doublethink phenomenon of pure fantasy' (1986: 175). According to Wood, the fantasy blockbusters of Lucas and Spielberg construct the adult viewer as childlike, which is part of what has stopped them being taken seriously. 'They work', he says, because 'I enjoy being reconstructed as a child, surrendering to the reactivation of a set of values and structures that my adult self has long since repudiated' (Wood 1986: 164). For Wood, the emphasis on spectacle and formulaic narrative structure of these fantasy blockbusters offers the audience pleasures which are both familiar and regressive. They mainly provide reassurance, 'don't worry, Uncle George (or Uncle Steven) will take you by the hand and lead you through Wonderland', before safely arriving at a happy end (Wood 1986: 165–6).

This argument is part of a criticism of the ideological content of Lucas and Spielberg's fantasy blockbusters which are seen to reflect President Ronald Reagan's America (1981–1989). Wood (1986) contextualizes the original *Star Wars* trilogy (1977–1983) in terms of US fears of fascism, nuclear anxiety and threats to patriarchal authority after a decade of liberation movements, and concludes that the films themselves support reactionary social values such as racism, sexism and homophobia. He argues that these reactionary ideologies are reflected in the handling of *Star Wars* characters like Princess Leia and C-3PO. Despite 'intermittent outbursts of activity' Leia's main function is 'to be rescued by the men, involving her reduction to helplessness and dependency' says Wood, and C-3PO is given an 'affected British accent' and 'effeminate mannerisms' which code the robot as a 'subordinate, subservient (and comic and timid) gay character' (1986: 173–4). *Star Wars* is thus regarded as a conservative fantasy because despite the fact that the story is about rebels who rise up against an oppressive Empire, there are no challenges made to dominant hierarchies of gender, sexuality or race. In Wood's view, 'the project of the *Star Wars* films and related works is to put everyone back in his/her place' (1986: 174).

Much is then made of fantasy being prevalent in 'Reaganite' cinema, the reoccurring themes of which were conservatism, escape, nostalgia and sentimentality. However it would not be accurate to claim that these or other blockbuster films only hold conservative connotations, and Michael Ryan and Douglas Kellner propose that 'a struggle between right-wing and left-wing uses of the fantasy mode is evident' (1990: 244). Consider Spielberg's films of the late seventies and eighties, for example. Ryan and Kellner (1990) pick out aspects of E.T. which are liberal and left-leaning. They say that the fantasy story is an 'ideal of social reintegration' told from a viewpoint of 'tolerance, empathy and acceptance' otherwise under threat in Reagan's America (Ryan and Kellner 1990: 261). Some scholars are more sceptical about the representation of the film's cute and loveable 'alien' though. In E.T. 'Spielberg constructs otherness as essentially sameness', writes Lester Friedman, 'We have met the Other, and he is just like us' (2006: 57). Or as Wood says, 'E.T. is one of us; he just looks a bit funny' (1986: 180).

Though people may argue about the relative ideological leanings of blockbuster fantasy, few would deny that the filmmakers often demonstrate vast amounts of technical skill. It is significant that the era of the blockbuster is also the era of the independent effects company. Lucas, in particular, is thought to have revolutionized special effects. By the 1960s the decline of the studio system caused the studios to close down the in-house effects departments that kept production going at a rapid pace. To create the state-of-the-art effects for *Star Wars*, Lucas set up his own facility and effects team called Industrial Light & Magic (ILM) in 1975, a division of his production company Lucasfilm. The technology ILM developed to make *Star Wars* was especially influential to the advancement of modern visual effects so prevalent in blockbuster fantasy films. For the first time computerized motion control systems were used in *Star Wars* to move cameras and models. This gave the spaceships a greater sense of scale, movement and realism, and enabled the creation of the spectacular space battle sequences that amazed cinema audiences. From this moment on, visual effects became 'at once more complex and less expensive to achieve than ever before' (Cook 2002: 384), they also became more common. In the 1970s and 1980s many other independent effects companies were established by artists and filmmakers in order to service the increased demand, such as Jim Henson's Creature Shop (founded in 1979) and Tippett Studios, founded in 1984 by former head of the ILM animation department Phil Tippett.

ILM regularly supplied effects to fantasy films by Lucas and Spielberg during the 1980s and 1990s, including the *Indiana Jones* franchise (1981–ongoing) which they collaborated on (Lucas produced, Spielberg directed). In addition ILM worked on a wide variety of notable fantastic productions such as *Who Framed Roger Rabbit?* (1988), *The Abyss* (1989), and *Terminator II: Judgement Day* (1991). Over the years the company notched up an impressive list of landmark technical firsts, from the first completely computer-generated sequence in *Star Trek II: The Wrath of Khan* (1982), to the first morphing sequence in *Willow* (1988), and the first digitally animated creatures produced to realistic effect were the ILM dinosaurs in *Jurassic Park* (1993). Above all, ILM played a vital role in the innovation and adoption of new digital technologies. Previously, computer graphics had a reputation for involving a great deal of time and expense, and for not looking real. The digital effects developed by ILM helped to change this, as evidenced by the domination of CGI in the contemporary film industry. The company has gone on to garner praise (and awards and nominations) for contributions to recent blockbuster fantasy franchises such as the *Harry Potter* (2001–2011) and *Pirates of the Caribbean* (2003–ongoing) films and, somewhat more controversially (we need only mention Jar Jar Binks), the *Star Wars* prequel trilogy (1999–2005).

Writing about technology in contemporary Hollywood cinema, Michael Allen explains that 'now that computer-generated effects are central to Hollywood's production methods, the independent effects-house model is very much the one being followed. Modern production methods have created "service differentiation" – specialist companies handling specific aspects of the production process' (1998: 125). This 'service differentiation' method is commonly used on Hollywood fantasy today, and the allocation of digital effects work is part of an increasingly transnational production system, where a film is likely to be worked on separately by a variety of specialist companies, often from all over the world. As a result the list of credits for a film like *The Chronicles of Narnia: Prince Caspian* (2008) includes effects by British companies Moving Picture Company (MPC) and Framestore CFC, Weta Digital and Weta Worksop based in Jackson's native New Zealand, and Giant Studios in America, among others. For instance, MPC designed the character Reepicheep including his facial features, body and fur; Framestore worked on the lion Aslan; and Weta (now a major player in special effects) updated technologies developed for *The Lord of the Rings* to create miniatures, costumes, weapons and armour for use in the film's spectacular battles sequences.

Of course, *The Chronicles of Narnia* (currently 2005–2010) is only one of many fantasy film franchises to come out of Hollywood in the 2000s. As we have already noted fantasy is currently a Hollywood favourite, some might say more so than science fiction which was strongly emphasized in the 1980s and 1990s. One of the most obvious economic advantages fantasy offers the big studios is that 'fantasies lend themselves to a broad range of merchandizing and fantasy fans tend to collect things' (Thompson 2003: 45). Again we can look to *Star Wars* to establish the precedent for this practice. In a historical account of 1970s American cinema David Cook describes *Star Wars* as 'the first true film franchise' because with it 'merchandising became an industry unto itself, and tie-in product marketing began to drive the conception and selling of motion pictures rather than vice versa' (2002: 51). In fact, the worldwide sales of *Star Wars* T-shirts, music, posters, models, action figures and other ancillary products far out-grossed the original box-office receipts. New market and cross-media opportunities mean that fantasy film franchises have become increasingly commodified since the release of the first *Star Wars* trilogy. Contemporary Hollywood is adept at creating synergies with merchandise and marketing tie-ins, and fantasy films are made into video games and theme park rides, which in turn are source materials for fantasy franchises. It is not surprising that Lucas (who famously retained the merchandising rights to the films as part of his deal with 20th Century Fox) has sought to maximize revenue by creating new *Star Wars* spin-offs and tie-ins (and film prequels), many fans say to the point of over-saturation.

In the conglomerate scheme of contemporary Hollywood, where the major studios are divisions of multinational corporations, we are now also accustomed to the concept of fantasy brands which extend across multiple media platforms and products. Robert Maltby discusses the growth of global multimedia 'megabrands' like The Lord of the Rings, Batman or Harry Potter, which fit well into the modern strategies of corporate Hollywood (2003: 211). The power of the Harry Potter brand and the largest conglomerate Time Warner provide a good example. In Brand Hollywood Paul Grainge (2008) explores the 'brand spectacle' of the Harry Potter phenomenon. Owned by Time Warner, the Harry Potter brand is carefully managed by Warner Bros. with the aim to 'create a long-term basis of corporate synergy' (Grainge 2008: 142). In addition to Warner Bros.'s planned eight film franchise based on the seven Harry Potter novels by J.K. Rowling, Time Warner has put to work its online, magazine, broadcasting and music subsidiaries to generate hype around the brand to great success. In 2005 it was reported that the first three films in the Harry Potter franchise (2001–2011) made £1 billion at the global box office, that there were over 400 items of Harry Potter merchandise available, and that the Harry Potter brand valuation was estimated at £2.2 billion (Simmons 2005). The same sort of phenomenon occurred with The Lord of the Rings trilogy, which also set all kinds of sales records and earned 'buckets of money' (Wasko 2008: 36) for New Line Cinema (Jackson and others), and ultimately, Time Warner.

Without the benefit of historical distance it is difficult to assess the shelf life of the current wave of high budget fantasy blockbusters, or the durability of the new media fantasy franchises that dominate the global box office. But, at the time of writing this chapter, new instalments of the Harry Potter, The Lord of the Rings and Pirates of the Caribbean blockbuster franchises are among those forthcoming, and this clearly affirms that fantasy has become very big business in the contemporary era, and that for now this phenomenon is still going strong.

SPECTACULAR TECHNOLOGIES

In key respects the associations established in the early years of film between magic, illusion, spectacle and storytelling continue to be employed today in the creation of fantasy. Lucas, Spielberg and their contemporaries use spectacular effects and types of illusion that are in many ways similar to the 'tricks' and techniques developed by pioneer filmmakers, such as Méliès, whose works have gone down in film history as precursors of modern fantasy (North 2008: 26). It is not however only the obvious techniques of special effects like CGI that fantasy filmmakers have depended on to draw us into the story world of the film. Other important technological breakthroughs include sound, colour, widescreen and DVD. Though storytelling is usually very much in evidence, Geoff King acknowledges that 'Spectacle tends to be foregrounded especially during periods of innovation' (2000: 31) when technologies such as these become an attraction for audiences. It follows that fantasy films will often showcase the new audiovisual techniques and technologies used to make them. And spectacular innovations in the making, distribution and exhibition of fantasy film are essential to realize the worlds in which the story unfolds. As King elsewhere comments, when we experience fantasy fiction presented so convincingly and yet so spectacularly on the screen, 'We are meant to say "wow", either silently or aloud, at least some of the time' (2006: 339).

Sound

Before the advent of sound cinema in 1927, many silent film shows were accompanied by forms of music (see Altman 2004). Some of the most prestigious films made in the silent era were sent out by the studios with full scores to be performed by orchestras in the bigger theatres. Early examples of silent fantasy films which were scored include Lang's two-part epic German expressionist fantasy Die Nibelungen, and the American made Arabian Nights adaptation The Thief of Bagdad (1924), starring Douglas Fairbanks. The original score to Die Nibelungen was written by Gottfried Huppertz, who also supplied the score to Metropolis (1927) for Lang. Similar to Die Nibelungen which we discussed above, The Thief of Bagdad is probably best known for its spectacular visual design, including elaborately stylized studio sets and fantasy effects such as a flying carpet, a flying horse and a dragon. But it is also significant that the original score to The Thief of Bagdad, composed by Mortimer Wilson, matches the action and setting of the story. Both films tell us that, even in the so-called silent era, sound already played a significant role in fantasy storytelling and the creation of atmosphere.

It is worth pointing out that the score is still an effective way of communicating the feel and themes of a film, and fantasy demonstrates how powerfully evocative the use of film music can be. Composers like Bernard Herrmann, John Williams, Danny Elfman, and Howard Shore are celebrated for their imaginative scoring of fantasy films such as *Jason and the Argonauts* (Herrmann), *E.T.* (Williams) and *Edward Scissorhands* (Elfman). Kevin Donnelly (2006) discusses Shore's original music for *The Lord of the Rings* which, he says, combines a traditional orchestra with a choir and songs performed by guest singers to develop sounds and themes that underscore the storyline, characters and action in the blockbuster trilogy. Of course, in the contemporary film industry, soundtrack albums have considerable commercial value too, and Donnelly notes that Shore's music for *The Lord of the Rings* was a 'consumer attraction' with an importance of its own (2006: 312).

The quality of sound and the technologies used to record and replay it are, without question, key issues in the history of film production and exhibition. Despite the obvious limitations that the arrival of bulky recording equipment imposed on the filmmaking process, fantasy adapted to the coming of sound. Made not long into the 'talkie' era, the use of new post-production processes in sound design contribute to the central illusion in *King Kong* and, in conjunction with groundbreaking visual effects, give life to O'Brien's stop-motion animated beast. Headed by Murray Spivak, RKO's sound department recorded and mixed three separate tracks together, one each for sound effects, dialogue and music score (composed by Max Steiner), onto a single master track which was then attached to the film. The use of sound effects in *King Kong* was particularly creative and experimental. To create convincing sound effects to accompany Kong, for instance, real animal noises were recorded, replayed backwards or slowed and layered to produce his distinctive roar (Morton 2005: 75–6). Plus, actress Fay Wray's scream is one of the most unforgettable sounds heard in *King Kong*, and indeed early sound cinema.

If the art of designing sounds can be traced back to 1930s cinema and films like *King Kong*, then, as Gianluca Sergi observes, improvements in recording equipment and reproduction systems mean that sound remains one of the defining features of film production and exhibition since the 1970s, and increasingly 'These sounds can often also stand as a "spectacle" in their own right' (2004: 153). Developments in surround sound technologies, such as the introduction of Dolby in the 1970s, THX in the early 1980s and digital sound in the early 1990s, give contemporary audiences high quality sound in the cinema and at home. In recent years fantasy film, like science fiction, has successfully applied these technical innovations, taking advantage of the spectacle of sound.

The impact of George Lucas and Lucasfilm in the pioneering of these technologies is yet again marked. In 1977 *Star Wars* was the first film both recorded and released in Dolby stereo. THX was developed by Lucasfilm to create a set of standards for sound playback. The aim was that these standards would improve the quality of sound in cinemas and allow sound designers to extend the range of sound effects, which would otherwise be lost on audiences. *Return of the Jedi* (1983) was the first film to be played in THX-certified cinemas in 1983. Sixteen years later, the new episodes in the *Star Wars* franchise also used improvements in digital sound, including the latest Dolby Digital Surround EX (Sergi 2004: 31), and recently the soundtrack to the original trilogy was digitally remastered. Though most critical attention tends to concentrate on the spectacular special effects in contemporary fantasy blockbusters, it is apparent that (big) atmospheric sound and music greatly adds to the spectacle and gives a heightened sensory experience, generating excitement, tension and emotion. In blockbuster series such as *Star Wars*, *The Lord of the Rings* and *The Chronicles of Narnia* sound design and presentation are just as important as visual elements to the making of fantasy story worlds and creatures.

Colour

The technical principles of colour, like those of sound, were known long before they became dominant in the film industry and fantasy, in particular, was closely associated with colour from the first days of cinema. We mentioned that Méliès, for example, had sections of frames hand-painted and individual colours were used as effects to enhance the spectacle of the image.

Early colour film processes were expensive and time-consuming and various techniques such as tinting, toning, and 'additive' (e.g. Kinemacolor) and 'subtractive' (e.g. Kodachrome) systems vied for adoption. Gunning describes colour in early cinema as a 'superadded quality' aimed at 'sensual intensity' which tended to overwhelm realism (1995: 253). In many early films colour was used for signification; however, it was a novelty rather than a standard and as a device it was, on the whole, regarded as artificial rather than naturalistic.

Today, we are so used to colour film that the idea that it appeared unrealistic to audiences might seem strange to us. As Edward Buscombe points out, 'We perceive the world as colored, after all, and therefore an accurate representation of it should also be colored' (1985: 88). But Buscombe then goes on to explain that, in line with critical debates about fantasy and realism in cinema, 'in fact it has never been a question of what is real but of what is *accepted* as real. And when it first became technically feasible, color, it seems, did not connote reality but the opposite' (1985: 88, emphasis in original). Tension between storytelling and spectacle was also a concern that held back the introduction of colour technology. The fear, in this case, was that attention to film colour would detract from the narrative.

Technicolor developed a two-colour system in the mid-1920s (based on the subtractive process), which was replaced in 1932 by a new three-colour format, resulting in a richer spectrum of colours and a greater intensity on film. In the 1930s the use of colour gradually became more common but was still perceived as unrealistic and Steve Neale notes that through the 1940s and 1950s, 'Colour was still overwhelmingly associated, aesthetically, with spectacle and fantasy' (2006: 19). In consequence Technicolor was used in Disney's first full-length animated features, such as Snow White and the Seven Dwarfs (1937) and Pinocchio (1940), and in big spectacular film productions such as Alexander Korda's 1940 version of The Thief of Bagdad, which also had fantastic sets and special effects.

Famously, Technicolor is made to function symbolically in sequences in The Wizard of Oz and A Matter of Life and Death (1946). The way that both these fantasy films, which bookend the Second World War, switch between monochrome and colour is comparable. In The Wizard of Oz, colour is used in the land of Oz, while Dorothy's home in Kansas is shot in monochrome (Figure 3.4). Here, the drabness of reality and everyday life is shown in the use of monochrome, in contrast with the vivid and rich colours of the section that signals fantasy for audiences. *A Matter of Life and Death* inverts this technique, however, and subverts the associations of colour: monochrome sequences are set in heaven (Figure 3.5) and Technicolor is used to depict Earth, specifically wartime Britain. In this way, the film contrasts the austere realm of heaven and eternity with the colourful experience of earthly life and love, which is itself a kind of romantic fantasy. In *A Matter of Life and Death*, an angel who arrives on Earth comments self-reflexively on the difference between these two worlds, saying 'One is starved for Technicolor up there'. Other films have since used the distinction between colour and monochrome as a way of creating a contrast between reality and fantasy, for example *Der Himmel über Berlin/Wings of Desire* (1987) and *Pleasantville* (1998).

Colour finally became the norm in film in the 1960s and, with a few exceptions, has mostly lost its unreal associations. Recently, technical advances in the practice of digital grading have, Scott Higgins (2007) says, given filmmakers more aesthetic and stylistic colour choices to make in post-production. In particular, Higgins notes the importance of *The Lord of the Rings* trilogy in the development of digital colour grading, using the software later named 5D Colossus (2007: 214–15). Digital grading was, for instance, used to achieve the intensely rich and bright oranges and greens of Rivendell and the Shire, symbolizing the rural ideal of these fantasy landscapes of Middle Earth (see Thompson 2008a). This new colour technology, like the majority of the innovations we discuss, offers significant spectacular and storytelling potential for fantasy film.

Widescreen and 3D

Widescreen is another technological development adopted by the film industry in the 1950s and added to stereo sound and colour to enhance spectacular fantasy. Before this time, widescreen was technically possible (some experimentation occurred during the 1920s and 1930s), but economic factors such as a downturn in profits and investment in sound, meant the

Figure 3.4   In *The Wizard of Oz* monochrome is used for scenes in the ordinary, everyday world of Kansas

Figure 3.5   The escalator that ascends to the monochrome afterlife world of heaven in *A Matter of Life and Death*

technology was not in general use. It took competition from television and declining cinema audiences for the industry to reintroduce widescreen as a new technology in film production and exhibition based on the advantages of size and scale. By this time, Maltby observes that, 'A movie had to become much more of a special event to draw its audience' (2003: 251). Widescreen processes and formats launched in the 1950s and 1960s include Cinerama, CinemaScope, Panavision, Vistavision, and Todd AO (see Belton 1992).

In 1952 the first widescreen films, made using Cinerama, were shot using three synchronized cameras and projected on to a wide concave screen that surrounded the audience. To begin with Cinerama films were usually non-fiction spectacular travelogues, so it is interesting to note that one of the system's first two fictional films is a fantasy, *The Wonderful World of the Brothers Grimm* (1962) co-directed and produced by George Pal (well known for his work on science fiction films in the 1950s and 1960s). Still, it would seem that fantasy was used as a vehicle for the spectacle of Cinerama rather than the other way round. 'Despite its title', Terry Staples says, *The Wonderful World of the Brothers Grimm* 'is not primarily about the Grimms. It is about Cinerama . . . In a Cinerama film the director's job was to exploit the system's ability to make the audience feel like they are at the very heart of the action' (2008: 142).

Ultimately though, the competing technology of CinemaScope was much better suited to the kinds of fictional films that Hollywood made: like Cinerama it enhanced spectacle and scale, but unlike Cinerama this did not so overwhelm realistic storytelling, nor was it as expensive for exhibitors. Characteristic of marketing in this period, the posters for the 1959 fantasy adventure *Journey to the Center of the Earth* advertise the main technological attractions which make this film a big screen experience. These novelty attractions include the use of special effects (to give '1001 Wonders!' and '1001 Thrills!'), the DeLuxe colour process and, of course, its widescreen presentation in CinemaScope.

With the development of new processes widescreen became standard, and though screen size is an attraction for contemporary audiences, today it takes a format like IMAX to hold real novelty and the spectacular value of cinema as an event. IMAX trades on its giant screen size, often stated as ten times bigger than a standard cinema. Fantasy blockbusters in particular lend themselves well to this format and in recent years several have been available in IMAX versions. In 2005 *Harry Potter and the Goblet of Fire* and *Batman Begins*, for example, both received a simultaneous IMAX and conventional theatrical release. Much like Cinerama, the aim of the IMAX experience is to immerse the audience, and in addition to the widest of widescreens and powerful digital sound, many IMAX films use 3D technology to create the extra spectacular illusion of depth.

Though there were a number of earlier experiments in 3D presentation, it was in the 1950s, with rival processes like Cinerama and CinemaScope, that 3D cinema first became popular in Hollywood. This popularity was, however, short-lived and the advent of widescreen cinema meant that by 1954 the 3D boom ended (Belton 1996: 265–6). Of subsequent attempts to revive 3D technology, the current interest in 3D films is the most sustained and far-reaching in scope. With new techniques in digital filming and projection and more venues, not only are more films being shot in 3D, some existing 2D films also get converted into the format. Fantasy features prominently in the growing list of blockbusters that can be watched in 3D, such as *Up* (2009), *How to Train Your Dragon* (2010) and *Alice in Wonderland* (2010), or the remakes of *Journey to the Center of the Earth* (2008) and *Clash of the Titans* (2010). Popular fantasy films re-released in 3D include *The Nightmare Before Christmas 3D* (2006) and *Toy Story 3D* (2009), and there are rumours of forthcoming 3D conversions of the *Stars Wars* series and *The Lord of the Rings* trilogy, among others (McGavin 2008: 22–3).

The combination of storytelling and spectacle that 3D films offer is always the subject of much popular and critical debate. The most anticipated 3D film of 2009 was James Cameron's *Avatar* (it was also shown in 2D). Though many critics praised *Avatar*'s (traditional) story, most stressed the advances Cameron made in the use of 3D effects and technology. *Avatar* also received many nominations and awards, including Academy Awards for Art Direction, Cinematography and Visual Effects. We may consider *Avatar* suggestive of what the 3D format can bring to fantasy, giving greater visual depth to the world on screen and bringing the viewer much closer to the action than 2D images can. Certainly, the commercial and critical success of *Avatar* has begged the question 'Will 3D change cinema forever?' Only time (and economics) will tell whether, perhaps by experimenting more with fantasy, this latest trend in 3D may continue and move further from the old gimmick of things leaping out of the screen to add new imaginative levels to our cinema-going experience.

Animation

Animation is, as scholars such as Paul Wells (1998, 2002) have shown, an influential medium in cinema history, with many important achievements. Not least among these is the fact that the creative possibilities and techniques for crafting an animated story world and/or characters enable the production of some memorable fantasy films. Though, inevitably, we are unable to explore animation in all its varied forms here (see Wells 1998 for this), its use and development in fantasy is distinguished in two main branches: 2D and 3D animation.

The relationship between fantasy and forms of animation dates back to experiments in early film: in France, Méliès used stop-motion animation to develop trick effects; Emile Cohl created surreal animated line-drawn figures in *Fantasmagorie* (1908), and in America Winsor McCay produced one of the first cartoon characters, an anthropomorphized brontosaurus in *Gertie the Dinosaur* (1914). Key breakthroughs in the traditional 2D animation process, involving hand-painted cels, were made by Walt Disney in the 1920s and 1930s. During this 'Golden Era', Disney introduced sound and colour to cartoons and used a multi-plane camera (which allowed several levels of artwork) and the technique of rotoscoping (where live-action is drawn over to create animation) in order to produce the illusion of depth and movement. In 1937 *Snow White and the Seven Dwarfs* was the first of many feature-length animations made by the studio to employ these techniques effectively. The aim of 'orthodox' animation in the Disney-style is to achieve a level of animated realism which traditionally limits the form's more subversive qualities in favour of the narrative and ideological codes and conventions of classical storytelling (Wells 1998: 35–7).

Nowadays, computer technology has brought in a new era of cartoon animation, resulting in a move from 2D to 3D animation, and the establishment of digital animation studios like Pixar (bought by Disney in 2006) and DreamWorks. However, digital tools have not entirely replaced traditional 2D animation and the two are sometimes combined, in the works of Hayao Miyazaki and Studio Ghibli for example. In films like *Mononoke-hime/Princess Mononoke* (1997), *Sen to Chihiro no kamikakushi/Spirited Away* (2001) and *Hauru no*

ugoku shiro/Howl's Moving Castle (2004), Miyazaki kept digital work to a mini-
mum, using conventional 2D animation to create fantasy story worlds in the
style of Japanese anime. Though the diversity of anime in Japan means that no
one figure or studio can, or indeed should, be taken to represent the form (see
Napier 2005), it is fair to say that the global impact and cross-generational
appeal of Miyazaki's animated films for Studio Ghibli currently make him one
of the best known and best regarded animators in the world carrying on the
legacy of 2D. Moreover, Miyazaki's animated films challenge, among other
things, the predominance of Western animation, and the idea that animated
cartoons are only for children.

It should be stressed that the field of animation encompasses much more
than the Disney or even anime-style cartoons with which we are all now likely
to be familiar. Other animation styles and techniques, often used as three-
dimensional special effects in fantasy films, include: puppet and model
animation, animatronics and, of course, digital animation. Whichever method
is used, and however fantastic, the goal of these animated creations is usually
to appear convincing and realistic, though they also function as a spectacular
attraction. Many classic fantasy films employ the technique of stop-motion
to animate objects and/or model figures, creating the illusion of lifelike
movement and (inter)action. For example, inspired by the pioneering effects
work of *King Kong* animator O'Brien, Harryhausen developed a system he called
'Dynamation' to create animated effects for epic adventure and mythological
fantasy such as *The 7th Voyage of Sinbad*, *Jason and the Argonauts*, and *Clash of the Titans*
(1981). Today, watched during any one of the many, regular appearances
these films make on our televisions, famous sequences like Jason's battle with
an animated army of skeleton warriors in *Jason and the Argonauts* (Figure 3.6)
are still a spectacular (if slightly old fashioned looking) part of the live-action
storytelling.

At times the combination of live-action and animation used in fantasy
might be intentionally surreal, as in Švankmajer's *Neco z Alenky*, where live-
action, puppetry and stop-motion create the unsettling experience of a
dreamlike Wonderland. More often, though, it is a way of drawing audiences
into the fantasy, and a (sometimes uneasy) balance is struck between
storytelling conventions and technological advances in animation. In the

Figure 3.6 Ray Harryhausen's stop-motion animated army of skeletons in *Jason and the Argonauts*

1980s, the latest developments in puppetry and animatronics were used in a group of fantasy films including *The Dark Crystal* (1982), which has an all-puppet cast, and *The NeverEnding Story* (1984) and *Labyrinth* (1986) which feature a combination of puppets, animatronics and human actors. In these now cult films the unfamiliarity of the fantasy story world is emphasized by the presence of animated characters, such as the evil Skeksis, Falkor the Luckdragon or Hoggle the Dwarf, who are usually its main (or, in the case of *The Dark Crystal* which has no human characters, sole) inhabitants. But however fantastic, strange and visually spectacular these creatures look, more often than not the pursuit of realism means that, as far as possible, technology and performance techniques give the characters the appearance of naturalistic life, thereby inviting audience engagement.

With the emergence of CGI has come the ability to bring three-dimensional photorealistic animated objects and characters to (virtual) life. This has produced a new level of verisimilitude not only in animated cartoons, but also in live-action fantasy where the use of CGI has proved especially revolutionary. Still, the look and feel of other forms of animation continues to influence the makers of fantasy films, and combinations of traditional 3D animation, such as puppets and models, and new CGI are also effective. For the effects in

El laberinto del fauno/Pan's Labyrinth (2006) Guillermo del Toro mixed some CGI with makeup and animatronics. The film and its fantastic creatures, including Pan the faun and a giant toad, were praised for their nightmarish efficacy. Looking ahead, if The Power of the Dark Crystal, the highly anticipated sequel to The Dark Crystal, ever makes it out of the long pre-production phase, then it is also reportedly set to use modern techniques like CGI and traditional animation methods like puppetry and animatronics to continue the legacy of the 1982 original.

CGI

In recent years fantasy has greatly benefited from new developments in digital imaging technologies. The pioneering research of Lucas and ILM in the 1980s and 1990s, and the appearance of computer-animated sequences and effects in live-action fantastic films like Tron (1982) and The Abyss, helped to pave the way for the first full CGA (computer-generated animation) features, such as Toy Story (1995) and Antz (1998). Since the late 1990s digital technology and aesthetic processes have attained improved levels of sophistication, enabling the creation of rich, textured and multilayered film images with the capacity for movement and expression. Digital technology threatens to overtake many of the traditional effects techniques used by the film industry, such as matte painting, rear projection and model animation (Allen 2003: 202–10). In economic and practical terms, the increased capacity of computers, new software and reduced costs means that digital imaging is put to numerous uses and CGI is now regarded as 'the cinematic standard in special effects' (Keane 2007: 61).

The period from 1989 to 1995 is referred to by Michelle Pierson (2002) as the early 'wonder years' of CGI, when digital imaging was, on the one hand, self-consciously showcased as a new special effects tool and a spectacular illusion for audiences to gaze at. On the other hand, she notes that the early CGI aesthetic aspired to realism and every effort was made to engage audiences (Pierson 2002: 63–136). The conflicts between, among other things, visibility and invisibility, incorporation and separation, real and unreal, and immersion and disruption, which bring about the dialectic identified by scholars like

Pierson, are a focal point for ongoing debates about CGI, not just in film criticism, but also in the film industry, the media and between viewers.

In the 2000s CGI is very much an attraction, but it is also increasingly used to construct story worlds without which there would quite simply be no film to watch. This is evident in many recent blockbuster fantasy franchises, such as *Harry Potter*, *The Chronicles of Narnia* and *The Lord of the Rings*, where CGI has been used to create settings, characters and effects that are considered magical, mystical or otherworldly. Constructing a convincing fantasy landscape was vital to *The Lord of the Rings*. Though the New Zealand landscape was already spectacular, with the help of CGI the locations transformed into the geography of Middle Earth. Even in blockbuster fantasy, which relies more and more heavily on CGI, the balance between the spectacle of the digitally created image and its storytelling function can and does vary. As such, Geoff King (2006) situates the advent and development of CGI within the context of historical debates about the mixture of spectacle and narrative in mainstream cinema. He claims 'This has always been the case in the history of Hollywood, the particular mix [is] variable according to the circumstances of specific conjectures' (King 2006: 352).

In contemporary film theory, the potential to create CG characters is commonly used as a means to explore the impact of digital technology on the industry and audiences, and debates about spectacle and realism (see Keane 2007: 60–5). Fantasy is one of the principal film genres in which CG characters appear. In live-action fantasy films, CG characters might be employed as extras (e.g. digital crowd and battles sequences), in stunt work (e.g. superhuman moves), or they may take the form of mythical creatures and monsters, like Draco the dragon in *Dragonheart* (1996) and Kong in the 2005 version of *King Kong*. The technology of performance capture, which uses a live actor's actual movements as a model for a 3D computer-generated character, has started to get used extensively in fantasy, usually with the aim of digital photorealism.

Notably, the CG character Gollum in *The Lord of the Rings* trilogy was created using performance capture from actor Andy Serkis, resulting in what is widely regarded as realistic and natural movements, particularly facial expressions. Many people agree that Gollum's role in *The Lord of the Rings* demonstrates the ability of CG to do more than provide spectacle. Not only is Gollum important to the story, he is also a believable and complex character with whom we might empathize, or perhaps even identify. This argument was highlighted when Serkis won an award at the MTV Movie Awards for his performance as Gollum in *The Two Towers* (and many fans and critics felt he should have been nominated for an Academy Award for Best Supporting Actor).

Not all CG characters are as well received as Gollum. For example, the characters in Robert Zemeckis's animated Christmas fantasy *The Polar Express* (2004), many of which were played by Tom Hanks using performance capture, were repeatedly described as 'creepy' by reviewers and critics. Based on the popular Japanese video games, the animated film *Final Fantasy: The Spirits Within* (2001), which was the first attempt to make realistic entirely CG human characters, also met with criticism of the 'hyper-real' artificiality of its virtual stars. For Barbara Creed, the ability to create a convincing completely CG human, also known as a virtual actor or synthespian, is nevertheless in the foreseeable future: 'Hollywood is confident that eventually the techniques will be perfected, so that the synthespian will be indistinguishable from a human actor' (2003: 166).

DVD

The final technology we consider in relation to fantasy is DVD. This seems a fitting way for us to bring this chapter to a close, because not only has DVD become a major source of revenue for the modern film industry, the technology also affects how just about every fantasy we discuss gets viewed in the home today. DVD technology is part of changing patterns of fantasy production and consumption and, though in some ways the distinctions between big screen cinema and small screen home viewing hold true, in other respects DVD film culture has redefined how fantasy is now offered and experienced.

Barbara Klinger (2006a, 2006b) examines the impact of DVD on film culture and home viewing since the 1990s and rightfully calls attention to some of the benefits for the reception of film in the home. She notes that: 'As part of a home theatre system, DVD, particularly widescreen DVD, appears capable of delivering cinema in a way that approximates the image and sound quality of the theatrical situation' (Klinger 2006b: 366). One of the benefits of this digital technology for the 'high tech' home viewer of a special effects fantasy film is its ability to approximate (if you own the 'right' equipment, e.g. HD TV, surround sound) the spectacular experience of cinema. In some cases a back-catalogue DVD may even improve on the visual or sound quality of the original theatrical release. Disney, for instance, sells the 2008 DVD release '50th Anniversary Platinum Edition' of *Sleeping Beauty* (originally 1958) by highlighting the spectacular quality of the new technology: 'See more than you've ever seen before through the magic of state-of-the-art technology and experience this groundbreaking film restored beyond its original brilliance in the way Walt envisioned it'. Here it is claimed that the DVD version exceeds the original, and the digital format restores the fantasy as it was first imagined by Disney himself.

In addition to the delivery of the main feature, Klinger goes on to discuss the importance of the exclusive supplementary content which the home viewer is given access to on DVD, such as commentaries, interviews, behind-the-scenes footage, and deleted scenes. She argues that this sort of material has a number of effects on film culture today, including a foregrounding of the 'magic' of filmmaking, and the increased flexibility and interactivity afforded to the viewer by 'remote viewing' (Klinger 2006b: 366–73). For fantasy fans and collectors, DVD box sets, special editions and special features might usefully (re-)contextualize a film in terms of its historical, cultural, directorial, generic, or other frameworks. A recent instance of this is the 2006 re-issue two-disc special edition DVD version of *The Wizard of Oz*, which includes special features such as documentaries that consider the film's making and legacy, original musical pre-recordings, home movies and archival materials. On fantasy DVDs the spectacular technology of effects is generally celebrated and extra features educate the viewer about how the fantasy illusion was accomplished. Not only can such DVD extras and editions enrich the viewing experience of a fantasy film, they might also extend it. This is literally the case for *The Lord of the Rings* trilogy, which has so far been released on various two-disc, limited edition, and extended versions of the original theatrical cut, thereby encouraging fantasy DVD collection, repeat viewings and film connoisseurship.

In the 2000s Blu-ray emerged as the standard format for high definition DVD. The Blu-ray format has far more storage capacity than traditional DVDs. This storage capacity makes room for more material on a single disc, and far superior picture and sound quality. The arrival of *Avatar* on Blu-ray in April 2010 was widely hailed as a coming of age for the new technology. Though the initial *Avatar* Blu-ray came without any special features (and no 3D), the release nevertheless broke the UK record for the biggest opening day sales of a Blu-ray film, and online review sites were universally enthusiastic about the as yet unrivalled technical quality of the high definition disc. It was reported that all the available space on the Blu-ray disc was used for the highest quality audio and video film transfer possible, making the viewing of the world of Pandora at home extraordinarily crisp and bright. Though cinema may never die, fantasy film is increasingly consumed in the home, and for those willing to buy into the latest technology Blu-ray represents another important step forward in the experience of these spectacular story worlds made for our screens.

4

'ONCE UPON OUR TIMES . . .': JOURNEYS IN CONTEMPORARY FANTASY FILM

In previous chapters we have examined the inheritance and role of fantasy storytelling in the medium of film; we also set out some key theoretical debates that relate to fantasy, and we considered the historical evolution of the industry and the technology of fantasy filmmaking. In this final chapter we highlight some specific films that give us insight into aspects of the politics of representation in fantasy, stylistic approaches to storytelling and the imaginative experiences of filmmakers and audiences. We do so in order to provoke further thought about the complex relationships between fantasy film, stylistic formal choices and/or issues of culture. As such, we continue to use representative examples from fantasy film, with which the reader is most likely to be familiar, and which in this case share the contextual background of contemporary cinema. This account has argued that the fantasy film is somewhere we may realize and manifest our hopes and fears, our wishes and imaginings, and is a magic mirror that can reflect back to us our dreams and visions, in some way transformed. The following case studies emphasize how some of the concerns raised in the rest of this book may overlap and influence each other and illustrate what this might tell us about the mirror modern-day fantasy films holds up to aspects of cinematic representation, culture and audiences.

This chapter is divided into five sections that use close textual analysis and film criticism to discuss the topic at hand. The first and second sections focus on how the hero and the monster are figured in select fantasy films, and the far from clear-cut views on the representation of gender, sexuality, race and disability to which they may connect. The third section comments on the classification issues raised by the portrayal of fantasy violence exemplified by films from the superhero cycle which have proved especially controversial in recent years. The fourth section looks at a revisionist trend in fantasy, where films playfully subvert traditions of fairy tale storytelling, though we join others who ask to what end? The last section foregrounds relevant films that respond to the contemporary preoccupation with time, and the fantasy appeal of temporal manipulation which can challenge our perceptions of time and space. The selection of fantasy films and topics in this chapter and elsewhere was guided by the goal of examining some key issues and ongoing debates, and it is hoped that these will inspire the reader to journey on and look beyond them to other fantasy films and topics of their own choosing.

FANTASY HEROES

Though the term hero can refer to the chief character in a fantasy story who is male or female, the majority of traditional heroes are men. It is telling that in *The Hero with a Thousand Faces* Joseph Campbell (1993 [1949]) structures his analysis around the mainly male hero monomyth that is the underlying pattern of numerous myths, legends, folktales and literature and recurs in many twentieth- and twenty-first-century fantasy films (and is sometimes directly applied in films such as *Star Wars*, 1977). Many popular fantasy films focus on the traditional male hero on a mythic or archetypal quest journey following the narrative trajectory set out by Campbell of separation, initiation and return, which we discussed in Chapter 2. The traditional male hero type reflects the culturally constructed ideal of masculinity based on physical strength and endurance, individualism and morality. Because the male hero embodies the most idealized qualities of a society his characteristics respond to changes over time, but in general he draws on and reinforces dominant notions of heterosexual white masculine privilege. In contemporary cinema (and culture), traditional male heroism has certainly not died out, but other notions of heroism have become successful and can challenge hegemonic stereotypes. In Hollywood fantasy, the original *Pirates of the Caribbean* film trilogy (2003–2007) is particularly fascinating, though not unproblematic, in this regard. In many ways the *Pirates of the Caribbean* films follow the typical Hollywood blockbuster formula, and they consciously evoke familiar character (stereo)types of the classic swashbuckler, including the male action adventure hero. But they also show how the classic fantasy adventure story is changed and adapted to make room for different kinds of heroes that arguably represent a (re)negotiation in traditional gender codes.

That the *Pirates of the Caribbean* film trilogy is often spoken of as a pirate fantasy adventure in the historical 'swashbuckler' genre is significant. In his work on the swashbuckler, Jeffrey Richards observes the influences of Romanticism, the historical novel and the model set by Sir Walter Scott on notable authors of swashbuckling fiction such as Alexandre Dumas and Robert Louis Stevenson (1977: 8–10). The basic characteristics of the classic cinematic swashbuckler would therefore typically include 'historical settings, gentlemen heroes and swordfights' (Richards 1977: 1), and an elaborate visual style predominates. On screen, Richards traces the swashbuckler back to the silent era when Douglas Fairbanks was best known for his dashing roles in *The Mark of Zorro* (1920), *The Thief of Bagdad* (1924) and *The Black Pirate* (1926), followed by the large-scale Hollywood productions featuring athletic, pin-up male stars like Errol Flynn and Burt Lancaster. On the romanticized figure of the swashbuckling film hero, Brian Taves paraphrases Richards (1977: 4–5) to explain:

> Swashbucklers stress the purity of the hero's motives, his physical and mental agility, impeccable manners, and often witty speech. The aristocracy in the swashbuckler is one of bearing rather than inheritance; whether a noble or a commoner, the hero is a gentleman and a patriot, with humor, charm, and gallantry underlying the devotion to justice.
>
> (1993: 18)

Though not specifically about Will Turner, this is a description that effectively sums up his character (perhaps minus the wit), introduced in the first *Pirates of the Caribbean* film. In the early sequences of *The Curse of the Black Pearl* (2003) apprentice blacksmith Will already has some of the archetypal qualities of the swashbuckling adventure hero: he can handle a sword deftly, and he is idealistic, honourable and brave. By the closing sequences not only has Will proven himself through his various heroic deeds, but he has also taken on the glamorous appearance of the romantic swashbuckler. In his last scene in the film Will exchanges his simple blacksmith's clothing for a feathered musketeer-style hat and colourful cape more reminiscent of the image of Flynn's eponymous hero in *Captain Blood* (1935). And played by Orlando Bloom, Will fulfils the requirement of 'male beauty and acrobatic skill' (Richards 1977: 4) needed to look and act like the typical swashbuckling hero in the lineage of Fairbanks and Flynn.

Will's story in *The Curse of the Black Pearl* follows the traditional hero's journey: when the kidnap of Elizabeth Swann causes him to leave Port Royal in order to go after the pirate ship the *Black Pearl* and rescue her from Barbossa and his undead crew to finally return home ready to do what he thinks is truly right. But Will is not the only character to go through such a heroic transformation arc, and though he is an obvious swashbuckler he is not the (only) main protagonist of the *Pirates of the Caribbean* film trilogy. In particular it is noted (e.g. Jesse-Cooke 2010: 214) that screenwriters Ted Elliott and Terry Rossio state that Elizabeth is the main character. Indeed this emphasis on the female character is not without precedent. Taves identifies that the pirate film has historically permitted 'some of the most important roles for women in the adventure genre', and with this in mind Elizabeth can be thought to join the ranks of a 'large number of fiery women of the sea' (1993: 29).

Certainly, Elizabeth is the first character we see in *The Curse of the Black Pearl*, and in a DVD commentary to accompany these opening scenes Elliott and Rossio say: 'Elizabeth is actually the protagonist of this story . . . the story is told from her point of view'. The issue of Keira Knightley's acting skills to one side, Elizabeth is given an increasingly strong role in the *Pirates of the Caribbean* film trilogy and it would seem reasonable to refer to her as a female (if not exactly a feminist) hero, and a modern woman for her time. It is interesting to note that editors Claudia Mitchell and Jacqueline Reid-Walsh (2008) make special reference to Elizabeth in the introduction to a two-volume encyclopaedia on contemporary 'girl culture' and popular media. Like other commentators and critics they reason that 'Knightley's "action hero" behaviour' in these films means that Elizabeth 'is presented not as a passive damsel in distress, but as a swashbuckling figure herself' (Mitchell and Reid-Walsh 2008: xxiii).

Throughout the original Pirates of the Caribbean story Elizabeth is portrayed as adventurous, intelligent, resourceful and independent. She begins The Curse of the Black Pearl fascinated by pirates, and as a young woman she rejects the rigid social conventions that govern her behaviour, symbolized by the restrictive corset she is laced into towards the start of the film. In fact, similar to Will's costume change described above, Elizabeth's clothing in the films often works with her development as a heroic female character, shifting from fashionable and expensive ladies' gowns to more male attire. When Elizabeth gets to speak what screenwriters Elliott and Rossio term her (self-confessedly 'cheesy') 'hero line' near the end of The Curse of the Black Pearl, she wears a Royal Navy uniform and takes an active role in fighting Barbossa's cursed crew. (Delivered by Elizabeth as she lances an undead pirate, the line explicitly refers to the constraints placed on femininity by period dress: 'You like pain?' she says as she swings a pole at him, 'Try wearing a corset'.) In some senses Elizabeth might then be considered to have something in common with transgressive cross-dressed female characters in films like Yentl (1983) and The Ballad of Little Jo (1993) where, as Yvonne Tasker points out, cross-dressing is 'presented as allowing female protagonists an opportunity and a freedom (of both physical movement and behaviour) that they would not otherwise achieve' (1998: 35, emphasis in original).

In Dead Man's Chest (2006) Elizabeth even manages to 'pass' successfully as a boy (though in the story world only). After she escapes from jail, she spends the majority of the film in male clothes, having disguised herself as a cabin boy on a merchant ship in order to go to Will's aid. Moreover by Dead Man's Chest Will has taught Elizabeth to handle a sword, making her better equipped to perform the role of heroic swashbuckler (in the first film she uses a variety of weapons including candlesticks, a pistol and a bedpan, but at no point does she actually fight with a sword). In At World's End (2007) Elizabeth's heroism is further tested when she is named a Captain, Lord and finally King of the pirates, and it is she who gets to make the rousing call to arms speech prior to the film's climactic sea-battle. However, the 'problem(s)' of the female action hero, theorized by feminist scholars such as Tasker (1993) and Sherrie Inness (1999), can also be seen in Elizabeth's transformation in the *Pirates of the Caribbean* trilogy. One criticism of her character might be that she only becomes 'equal' with the men in the story by appearing (e.g. costume) and behaving (e.g. violence and aggression) like them. We may ask whether femininity is used as a source of agency (and heroism) in the films. It would seem that the issue of whether a character like Elizabeth ultimately challenges or merely reinforces gender stereotypes remains up for debate.

Of course, by far the least straightforward (and the most intriguing) 'hero' figure in *Pirates of the Caribbean* is Captain Jack Sparrow. Though *The Curse of the Black Pearl* used the blockbuster approach to production, the less than favourable response to other recent pirate movies (such as *Cutthroat Island*, 1995 and *Treasure Planet*, 2002) meant the first *Pirates of the Caribbean* film was widely considered a surprise hit in the summer of 2003 (see Denison 2004). Three years (and two instalments) later, Nick Roddick reflects that *The Curse of the Black Pearl*:

> owed almost everything to what began as an extended cameo but grew to take over the picture: Johnny Depp's performance as Captain Jack Sparrow. I could be wrong, but I don't think this was part of the original game plan – the original *Pirates* featured snippets of Depp but focused mainly on special effects and Geoffrey Rush. The film, however, belonged to Depp.
>
> (2006: 10)

Whether they love or loathe the blockbuster franchise based on the Walt Disney theme park attraction, most critics and audiences agree that it is thanks to Captain Jack that *The Curse of the Black Pearl* was a success. His part in the story has grown accordingly (to the extent that the upcoming fourth film *On Stranger Tides* will further his adventures), and of all the characters Depp's interpretation of Captain Jack excites much keen discussion (especially on the Internet) about his appeal.

A popular theory is that his ambiguity is a major part of what makes Captain Jack both memorable as a character and problematic as a hero. In fact, there has always been a certain amount of moral ambiguity expected from the classic pirate film. Taves observes that: 'Even when cast in the heroic mold, pirates are not as clean living, patriotic or moral as most other adventurers, and they are allowed greater deviation from the norms of gentlemanly behavior' (1993: 27). This haziness about the concept of heroism and the pirate adventurer is exemplified and exaggerated by Depp's Captain Jack, and in *Pirates of the Caribbean* it is never really clear who he may side with at any given time. ('Whose side is Jack on?' Elizabeth asks at one point in *The Curse of the Black Pearl*. 'At the moment?' is Will's uncertain response.)

From one point of view, Captain Jack does perform some classically heroic actions for the benefit of others. In *Dead Man's Chest*, for instance, he dives into the sea to rescue Elizabeth from drowning, and he also (temporarily) forfeits his own quest for immortality towards the close of *At World's End* when he helps Will, who has been mortally wounded, to stab the heart of Davy Jones and become the new Captain of the Flying Dutchman. But from another point of view, Captain Jack constantly switches from ally to rival in his relationships with Will, Elizabeth and others, and most of his schemes are in pursuance of self-interested motivations at almost any cost. This is illustrated by any one of a number of double-crosses, dispossessions and deceptions instigated by Captain Jack against just about every character who makes some sort of an 'accord' with him over the course of the films. Like the magical compass in Captain Jack's possession (Figure 4.1), which constantly shifts to point to what

Figure 4.1   Captain Jack Sparrow follows his magical compass in the *Pirates of the Caribbean* film trilogy

he wants most instead of the permanently fixed point of magnetic North, his moral compass is based more on the way he interprets the 'guidelines' of the pirate code than on conventional social morality.

Many people therefore consider Captain Jack a prototypical fantasy anti-hero. In behind-the-scenes interviews producer Jerry Bruckheimer describes Captain Jack as 'heroic in a kind of underhanded way', and screenwriters Elliott and Rossio comment that they based his characterization on the trickster archetype. In essence Carl Jung (2010 [1959]) saw the trickster as a rebel against society's rules, tending to use deception to achieve goals. Similar to Han Solo in *Star Wars*, who also epitomizes the outlaw and anti-hero, Captain Jack occupies a (exciting) grey area somewhere between good and bad (Petersen 2009: 84). In past swashbuckling film cycles Richards says that:

> Outlaws, highwaymen, pirates . . . became steeped in an aura of popular myth. Their bold adventures, devil-may-care style of life, freedom of movement, easy wealth, made them objects of admiration and identification, escape figures from the harshness and monotony of everyday life.
>
> (1977: 8)

The *Pirates of the Caribbean* films are self-reflexive about this process of mythologization and celebrate the freedom from responsibility that an anti-hero like Captain Jack represents. Captain Jack's genius for self-mythologizing is the source of much humour across the series, from his legendary escape from an island on the backs of sea turtles, to his parting catchphrase 'This is the day you will always remember as the day you almost caught Captain Jack Sparrow!' And it is largely by association with him that other characters such as Will and Elizabeth come to realize their inner pirate too, transforming to become freer, more rebellious, and more adventurous than they were previously. Furthermore, outside the story world Captain Jack has proved extremely popular with audiences, who can use licensed merchandise and tie-ins to role-play, collect, read about or even dress up as the notorious pirate anti-hero (see Jesse-Cooke 2010).

Captain Jack's ambiguity also extends to his playfully subversive gender characteristics and sexuality. It is well known that the Disney executives were not especially pleased when they first saw Depp's eccentric portrayal of the masculine pirate, who was apparently originally imagined more in the style of Lancaster's rugged and handsome Captain Vallo in *The Crimson Pirate* (1952). Instead Depp famously modelled elements of his performance on influences such as aging rock star Keith Richards and the womanizing cartoon skunk from *Loony Toons* Pepé le Pew, and Captain Jack's signature costume, hair and makeup include a tricorne hat, various rings, beads and bangles, dreadlocks, kohl-black eyeliner and gold teeth. The actor also brought an unconventional set of traits to the role, like slurred speech, a slight stagger, and affected mannerisms. Leslie Felperin suggests that the studio was nervous because 'It was feared Johnny Depp's campy turn as the pirate Jack Sparrow would seem too effeminate, too drugged, or just too mannered for mainstream tastes' (2006: 65), though in the end audience responses to the character proved otherwise. In key respects the colourful reputation and ambiguous image of Captain Jack functions in contrast to the more clean-cut 'straight' male heroism of Will (Petersen 2009: 85). For Harry Benshoff and Sean Griffin Captain Jack is one of a number of male characters in early twenty-first century cinema who may cause us to question traditional ideals of masculinity and who perhaps 'represent a new negotiation in hegemonic masculinity' (2009: 300).

FANTASY MONSTERS

What is a fantasy hero without a monster to confront, contain or even destroy? Some fantasy monsters in film come from other magical and mythical worlds, some are manufactured by us, and others symbolize our inner desires, struggles and fears. In film studies the figure of the monster has received most attention in horror scholarship, where critics such as Robin Wood (1986) make connections between monsters and basic psychological, socio-cultural and political structures of repression, suppression and oppression. For Wood the monsters in horror are coded as racial, ethnic, sexual and ideological Others that come into conflict with the conservative norms of the dominant social order. The horror film thereby expresses 'our collective nightmares . . . [where] normality is threatened by the Monster' (Wood 1986: 78). Horror monsters are also approached as allegorical expressions of contemporary social, political and moral fears, threats and anxieties from specific eras, like nuclear terror in the 1950s, the monstrous family in the 1980s, and the AIDS crisis in the 1980s and 1990s.

Fantasy monsters likewise express ideas of Otherness and difference, based on the representation of race for example. Popular genre film, especially the fantastic genres, has represented changing concepts of race and ethnicity in complex and often contradictory ways. Ed Guerrero explains:

> the social construction of race, *otherness*, and nonwhiteness is an ongoing process, working itself out in many symbolic, cinematic forms of expression, but particularly in the abundant racialized metaphors and allegories of the fantasy, sci-fi, and horror genres. This practice can be explained by several mutually reinforcing factors including these genres' dependence on *difference* or *otherness* in the form of the monster in order to drive or energize their narratives; the now vast technological possibilities of imagining and rendering all kinds of simulacra for aliens, monsters, mutant outcasts, and the like; and the infinite, fantastic narrative horizons and story worlds possible in these productions.
>
> (1993: 56–7, emphasis in original)

Guerrero goes on to make the point that many of the films in these fantastic genres 'offer quite sharp countercultural critiques of the dominant social policies and values of the present' (1993: 57), and we will return to this argument shortly, but first let us examine how these representational conventions might tend towards conservatism. An alternative or secondary world fantasy like Peter Jackson's *The Lord of the Rings* film trilogy (2001–2003) is a prominent example of how fantasy in particular may allegorize race relations, and how contemporary audiences, critics and the media can read the monster in terms of racial coding, negative stereotyping, and relationships to real world hierarchies of power and difference.

Whether or not *The Lord of the Rings* was intended to comment on actual racial politics, many point out the apparent metaphorical function of race and colour-coding in the story world of Middle Earth. Generally speaking, the monstrous army of enemy races gathered by the evil Lord Sauron are characterized by darkness in contrast to the mostly (and, in the case of the Elves, spectacularly) white allies of the good Fellowship of the Ring. This is made especially clear by the heavy emphasis placed on (male) militarism in the film versions of *The Lord of the Rings*, and the long and impressive battle sequences staged by Jackson (using computer animation to generate thousands of characters). In the second and third films in the trilogy Gandalf the White (formerly Grey) and Aragon heir to the throne of Gondor lead coalitions to defend the racially white people of Rohan in the Battle of Helm's Deep and the symbolically white fortress city of Minas Tirith, against invasion from various non-white racial and cultural Others, including dark-skinned Orcs and Uruk-hai of Isengard and Mordor, corrupt Black Riders or Nazgûl, and savage non-Western Southrons and Easterlings. In this way the films appear to rest on binary oppositions like white and black, West and East, self and Other, and light and dark, to express the mythic theme of good versus evil, with most heroes and monsters clearly drawn.

It is hardly surprising, then, that a number of commentators find the racial politics of Jackson's *The Lord of the Rings* trilogy problematic, to say the least. For Sue Kim (2009) *The Lord of the Rings* films make evident some of the issues with our understanding of race. In her view, racial coding makes *The Lord of the Rings* 'the only contemporary fantasy/sci-fi blockbuster film series as immediately cringe-inducing as the first new *Star Wars* film, *Episode 1: The Phantom Menace*' (Kim 2009: 95), where alien characters like Jar Jar Binks and Watto seem to invoke negative racial stereotypes. In the build-up to the cinema release of *The Two Towers* in 2002 John Yatt unequivocally stated his opinion in the *Guardian* newspaper that '*The Lord of the Rings* is racist'. 'White men are good', says Yatt (2002), '"dark" men are bad, orcs worst of all'. Though makeup, prosthetics and effects technology mean that there is variation among them, the overall coding of the Orcs in the film trilogy brings together stereotypical signifiers of race and class. On screen the Orcs chiefly appear in (expendable) tribal masses: they are grotesque-looking and vicious green- and grey-skinned Others clad in dark scraps of clothing and crudely cast armour, they often speak with working-class Cockney accents, and their attitude and behaviour is uncivilized, violent and brutal.

Of all the monsters of Middle Earth, Jackson's portrayal of the Uruk-hai attracts some of the most attention as being racially suspect. The Uruk-hai are a type of Orc (crossed with 'Goblin-men') that the films show Saruman breed in the deep industrial pits underground at Isengard. His 'fighting Uruk-hai' are manufactured for use as an advanced army since they are physically large and powerful, they know no pain or fear, and they have a singular purpose to serve the will of Saruman. Because they are generally also massed and unnamed, the Uruk-hai are easily read in the tradition of racist caricatures in film of the primitive black beast. Though there are a few notable Uruk-hai characters created specifically for the film trilogy, they may confirm rather than counter the racial stereotype. For example, Lurtz is the first of Saruman's Uruk-hai seen to emerge fully formed from a muddy membrane (Figure 4.2). On this particularly monstrous origins scene in *The Fellowship of the Ring* (2001), Sean Redmond comments that 'The sheer size, strength and ethnic identity of this man-beast are quickly established. Shot in close-up, his blazing nostrils, dreadlock hair and animalistic posturing directly recalls the stereotype of the all-body/no-brain black buck of racist imagination' (2008: 97).

It is also potentially significant that in *The Fellowship of the Ring* the Uruk-hai leader Lurtz is played by New Zealand-born Maori actor Lawrence Makoare. (Makoare plays two other evil characters in *The Return of the King*, the deformed Orc leader Gothmog and the Nazgûl Witch King.) For Kim (2009) this is one of the more disturbing (type)casting choices made by the filmmakers that, albeit inadvertently, connects these fantastic representations to the discourses of historical (colonial) and current race relations in New Zealand and other cultures. In her view:

Figure 4.2 The monstrous newborn Uruk-hai warrior Lurtz in *The Lord of the Rings: The Fellowship of the Ring*

> the film simply overflows with racial issues that work at two levels. On the
> surface, the rhetoric of liberal multiculturalism – of many species living
> together in happy harmony – reassures us; at the same time, the spectre
> of whites besieged by dark hordes speaks to deeper racial anxieties.
>
> (Kim 2009: 99)

It is worth noting though that Redmond argues there is a critique of whiteness in The Lord of the Rings, and that hyper-white characters like Saruman (and even ethereal Elves Arwen and Galadriel) demonstrate that 'too much whiteness . . . is a dangerous, ultimately destructive subjectivity' (2008: 91).

Of course, the many races of Middle Earth represented in Jackson's film adaptation of The Lord of the Rings were mainly based on descriptions in J.R.R. Tolkien's book. Though Tolkien always denied that his work was either allegorical or topical, from when The Lord of the Rings was published in the 1950s scholars have suggested that it can be read as an allegory for the world wars that had recently ended and the new threat of nuclear weaponry. At the start of the twenty-first century critics see in Jackson's film trilogy a range of topical socio-political messages about the contemporary era, including a cautionary warning about the dangerous implications of genetic engineering (represented by Saruman's monstrous Uruk-hai) and a reflection on the Bush administration's war against terrorism. For Douglas Kellner the battle between the heroic forces of good and monstrous forces of evil in the films must be read in this modern context: 'In an era of the Terror War, The Lord of the Rings film cycle enjoins patriarchal and crusading militarism that reflects Bush's crusade against terrorism and a post-2005 as-yet-not-articulated-crusade-against-tyranny' (2006: 38).

In the introduction to Framing Monsters: Fantasy Film and Social Alienation Joshua Bellin contends that 'fantasy films play a more fundamental part in the construction, dissemination, and maintenance of prejudice than is commonly admitted' (2005: 13), and the aim of his study is to reveal these ideological workings and demonstrate 'a long standing (and ongoing) tradition in fantasy film that identifies marginalized social groups as monstrous threats to the dominant social order' (2005: 2). In contrast to The Lord of the Rings trilogy, which possibly reinforces such negative stereotypes, is a fantasy film like

Tim Burton's *Edward Scissorhands* (1990) which we will discuss (and which Bellin himself uses to suggest how certain films may challenge the audience's 'ways of seeing', 2005: 167). Certainly, *Edward Scissorhands* has a distinct outlook on the monster theme. Like the Orcs and the Uruk-hai that Saruman manufactures in *The Lord of the Rings*, the eponymous Edward is also an unnatural Frankensteinian creation. And yet in *Edward Scissorhands*, played by Johnny Depp, the seeming monster is misunderstood, and the fairy tale-like story invites the audience to reflect on our social and cultural fears of difference.

At the beginning of *Edward Scissorhands* Edward is found by local Avon representative Peg Boggs living alone in the attic of a gothic-style mansion. The sequence where Peg meets Edward hiding deep in the shadows of the attic is particularly interesting in the way cinematic techniques such as *mise-en-scène* and music play on audience familiarity with the monster movie and cue expectations about his character, only to undercut them. The scene is shot mainly from the point of view of Peg, whose first negative reaction to Edward (like ours) is affected by the dark and forbidding inside to the rundown house on the hill, despite the beautifully sculpted topiary outside hinting that everything is not what it seems. The score (by Danny Elfman) becomes more ominous and menacing when Edward starts to move forward and for a brief moment evokes modern horror music of the slasher genre. Looking into the shadows we, like Peg, can make out an odd-looking figure with some weapon-like blades, and her reaction is to back away fearfully, saying 'I can see that I have disturbed you. How stupid of me. I'll just be going now'. This fear does not abate when Edward steps out of the shadows because his appearance is so irrevocably Other: he is peculiarly pale and scarred, he is dressed in tight black leather and latex, and of course, he has scissor hands (Figure 4.3). But when Edward speaks, the fear and suspense the scene has built-up unexpectedly halt, instead replaced with sadness and sympathy. 'Don't go' he responds timidly to Peg, and 'I'm not finished' he says in order to explain his physical difference. With this sequence begins the lesson not to judge by appearances alone, and Peg very quickly resolves 'I think you should just come home with me'.

Edward's experience of the pastel-coloured world of suburbia just beyond the gates of his darkly expressionist gothic home goes through two distinct

Figure 4.3   The Otherness of Edward in *Edward Scissorhands*

phases that both show how much he stands out from 'normal' society. At first, he is mostly welcomed by Peg's female neighbours who view him as a curiosity, and for a time his individuality and creativity mean that he seems popular with the local community who (with the exception of the Boggs family) otherwise appear to be living depthless and empty lives. Edward swiftly transforms the look and feel of the cookie-cutter neighbourhood by using his scissor hands to cut hedges, dogs and ladies' hair into all sorts of fantastic shapes and styles. His difference is even the source of some sexual excitement for stereotypical bored housewife Joyce who fantasizes, 'Do you imagine those hands are hot or cold? And just imagine what a single snip could do' ('Or undo!' sniggers her friend). But intolerance of Edward's Otherness soon rises to the surface and his innocence and social awkwardness are used against him to fuel prejudices. When Joyce's sexual advances get rejected by a confused Edward, she spreads the rumour that he tried to rape her. He also gets in trouble with the police for a robbery he is tricked into, and when he accidentally cuts Peg's son's face having saved him from getting run over by a van, the angry neighbours gather to chase Edward who finally retreats back to his hill-top isolation.

Edward can be linked to a long tradition of outcasts in storytelling, literature and film who in some way do not fit into dominant social groups (see Warner 1995: 313). In the DVD commentary Burton compares the suburban neighbours of *Edward Scissorhands* to the angry villagers of James Whale's *Frankenstein* (1931). This comparison is telling because in spite of appearances we learn that the true monster of the film is not really Edward at all, but rather the supposedly 'civilized' community who make him a scapegoat and project onto him their own fears and insecurities. For Bellin Edward is a 'freak' monster who:

> challenges the viewer's viewing not only by revealing the limitations of communal judgement but by closing the distance and upsetting the difference between the normal (who looks) and the freak (who is looked at). For when the freak looks, the performance of normalcy – including the act of freak gazing – becomes, in and through his eyes, the greatest freak show on earth.
>
> (2005: 190–1)

Other critical interpretations of Edward's difference include the alienation of subcultural youth (Markley 2007), racial conflict (Greene 1998: 146–7) and even the 'monster queer' (Benshoff 1997: 266), as well as the artistic outsider typified by Burton himself (Bassil-Morozow 2010: 68–9).

On an emotional level Edward's scissor hands act as an obvious metaphor for feeling like an outsider. Says Burton of the drawing he did as a teenager that the script of *Edward Scissorhands* was based on: 'It came subconsciously and was linked to a character who wants to touch but can't, who was both creative and destructive – those sort of contradictions can create a kind of ambivalence' (in Salisbury 2000: 87). The bittersweet ending that sees Edward return to his social alienation, following an unfortunate but necessary act of violence, serves as a final emphasis of the film's critique of popular attitudes towards Otherness and cultural difference.

FANTASY VIOLENCE

The representation and regulation of fantasy violence on our screens often proves contentious. When *Edward Scissorhands* was released in 1991 some violence in the final fight sequence was cut in order that the film could obtain a PG certificate in UK cinemas. Though there were no cuts made to *The Lord of the Rings*, only *The Fellowship of the Ring* was rated PG in the UK. The second and third instalments in the trilogy were both passed at 12A because they were considered darker than the first film, particularly the battle violence and the fantasy horror of monsters like the Black Riders, Orcs and Uruk-hai. Since the introduction of the 12A certificate in 2002, the British Board of Film Classification (BBFC) reports on the Student BBFC website (www.sbbfc.co.uk) that in general 'Films classified "12A" are the most complained about decisions', and many find the category controversial. In recent years some of the biggest fantasy blockbusters have been classified 12A, including the *Harry Potter* series from *Harry Potter and the Goblet of Fire* (2005) onwards, the first and third instalments in the *Pirates of the Caribbean* trilogy, *Indiana Jones and the Kingdom of the Crystal Skull* (2008), and many of the films in the new cycle of superhero adaptations. For example, *Spider-Man* (2002) and its sequels (2004, 2007), *The Spirit* (2008), *Hellboy* (2004) and its sequel (2008), and *Batman Begins* (2005) followed by *The Dark Knight* (2008) were all passed by the BBFC at 12A. The volume and levels of the violence in these superhero films is a hot topic in the media precisely because of their fantasy nature, and the fact that they appeal to younger audiences. These issues and more are picked up on in this discussion about fantasy violence, focused primarily on the high profile public response to *The Dark Knight*.

The tone of Christopher Nolan's *The Dark Knight* is, as the title suggests, unremittingly dark and the underlying theme that power corrupts is a long way from the simple good versus evil plots of past Batman films in the 1980s and 1990s. Most commentators and critics note the connections between new versions of classic superhero stories and characters like Batman and Spider-Man and concerns faced in contemporary culture, including the events of 9/11 and violent crime (e.g. Dawson 2008). It is therefore interesting that the storyline of *The Dark Knight* directly calls into question whether Batman is an answer to Gotham's problems or just another symptom of the failure of the law, and that the portrait of his persona is psychologically complex (and dark) rather than idealized. Batman's moral ambiguity, the character of the Joker and violence, are key factors that caused complaint about *The Dark Knight* in Britain, because the 12A certificate gives adults the right to take children younger than 12 to see the film at the cinema should they choose. With regard to violence, The Dark Knight comes with the consumer advice warning that the film 'Contains strong fantasy violence and sustained threat'. The extended classification information further explains that, in accordance with current guidelines, elements such as the fantasy context and the lack of detail or emphasis on injuries and blood meant the film received its 12A classification from the BBFC.

There was a great deal of media coverage on The Dark Knight in the summer of 2008, including much negative press about the classification. Many felt strongly that the tone and content was too violent for a 12A. Daily Mail columnist Allison Pearson (2008) criticized the BBFC, saying that 'Any board which can deem this film suitable viewing for children lacks the moral faculties to be any kind of judge at all', and in The Telegraph Jenny McCartney (2008) condemned 'a Hollywood intent upon mining the profit margin from barbarism'. British politicians joined the debate. An open letter that former Conservative leader Iain Duncan Smith wrote to The Times is quoted in full:

> Sir, On Sunday evening, I went with my 15-year-old daughter to watch *The Dark Knight*, the new Batman film. I was astonished that the British Board of Film Classification (BBFC) could have seen fit to allow anyone under the age of 15 to watch the film. Unlike past Batman films where the villains were somewhat surreal and comical figures, Heath Ledger's is a brilliantly acted but very credible psychopathic killer, who extols the use of knives to kill and disfigure his victims, during a reign of urban terrorism, laced with urban torture. It is a relentlessly violent film, filled with dark themes, and as I left I wondered what the board could possibly be thinking. There is no way that a parent could have been guided by the classification and realised what they were about to see.
>
> I am not complaining about the film: I enjoyed it and thought it very well made. My concern is that the board seem to have caved in to commercial pressures and forgotten that there is a protective purpose to the classification system.

(2008: 23)

This letter, the substance of which is representative of much of the controversy over the film classification in Britain, views the aesthetic style of *The Dark Knight* as less fictional and cartoonish and more brutal and believable. Such criticism, not of the entertainment value of *The Dark Knight* (which he confesses to enjoy), but of the BBFC and the effect that watching the film may have on a young audience, raises some important concerns about the assessment of fantasy violence in general; like where does fantasy violence end and realistic violence begin (and vice versa)?; how significant is context?; and what are the effects of violent imagery in fantasy film, particularly on children? In America *The Dark Knight* was given a PG-13 rating by the Motion Picture Association of America (MPAA). Like the BBFC the MPAA warned that the film includes 'violence and some menace' and the US media reported that some filmgoers felt the story was 'too dark for kids' (Bowles 2008).

In addition to the dark themes and tone of *The Dark Knight*, debates about the violence refer to sequences which some found especially strong in light of the 12A or PG-13 ratings. These include several scenes where the Joker threatens people with a knife, the Joker's 'pencil trick' scene, and the interrogation scene between Batman and the Joker. Clearly there are different ways to examine the representation of such violent sequences. One way is to think about the affective impact of how the violence is depicted. For example, when the Joker makes a sharp pencil 'magically disappear' by slamming a mobster's head down on it, his punch line, 'Ta-da! It's gone', makes for black comedy. This is in contrast to the scenes when the Joker harms more innocent characters (like Rachel Dawes), especially when the audience sympathizes with them. Alternatively we might stress what is or is not visible on screen: similar to the infamous scene with the pencil where the Joker kills a mobster, when Batman attacks the Joker in an interrogation room at the police station, graphic violence is implied but not actually shown. It is also useful to look at character and motivation: though *The Dark Knight* is not a simple good versus evil story and Batman is a flawed hero in a morally confused world, he is still our 'good guy' protagonist and this influences how we view his sometimes sadistic acts of violence. By contrast the Joker is driven by no motive other than to use violence to create anarchy for the sake of it, and however entertaining his character represents criminality and chaos. In fact, one of the biggest concerns voiced about The Dark Knight at the time (see above) was the threat of the Joker character and the intense performance by the late Heath Ledger.

In the UK, the Joker's fondness for knives was contextualized by the topical issue of rising teen knife crime, and one major retailer removed badges featuring the character from sale following claims that this merchandising further endorsed and glamorized using knives as weapons. Such arguments about the negative effects of fantasy violence on society are typical of those covered in the ongoing 'media violence debate', which the press often portrays as binaristic, but most researchers suggest is actually more complicated (Carter and Weaver 2003: 15–16). It is worth noting at this point that The Dark Knight itself comments on violence, and alludes to aspects of the effects debate. The film begins by introducing the problem that Batman's success at fighting crime in Gotham has inspired numerous imitators. These 'Batmen' are vigilantes who dress like Batman and model their violent behaviour on him. The Batmen are then a copycat phenomenon presumably led to commit acts of violence in response to media coverage of Batman's heroism, a play on the usual assumption that violent crime in the media directly leads to violent crime in real life. Later on in the film, the Joker's story of how he got his scars appears to support claims for the significance of psychological and social factors on violence. The Joker states that his father was 'a drinker and a fiend' who he witnessed beat up his mother and who took a knife to the face of his young son. From this version of the origins of the Joker's scars we may reason that the trauma of childhood abuse and a violent upbringing explains his violent criminality and close relationship to knives. But when the Joker tells a second version of the scar story (Figure 4.4) that is markedly different from the first the authenticity of this explanation is undercut and uncertainty is introduced. In the new version of his violent history, the Joker says that his scars are a result of self-mutilation in response to the violence of others. In The Dark Knight the Joker tells these violent stories to manipulate his audience, and his competing claims leave us with many more questions than answers.

Violence is certainly not new to fantasy or to storytelling. In a recent study which examines the current and historical debates about media violence David Trend observes that 'For centuries violence has been an important element

Figure 4.4   The Joker tells a version of the story of his scars when threatening Rachel Dawes with violence in *The Dark Knight*

of storytelling, and violent themes appear in the classical mythology of many nations, masterpieces of literature and art, folklore and fairy tales, opera and theatre' (2007: 3). Of course, debates about media violence not only consider the possible bad or harmful effects, but also note other functions. Of fairy tales, for example, Trend says that they 'warn children about the violent consequences of not behaving as instructed by adults' (2007: 3).

As discussed in Chapter 1, child psychologist Bruno Bettelheim is best known for his argument in *The Uses of Enchantment: The Meaning and Importance of Fairy Tales* (1991 [1976]) that fairy tales can provide a therapeutic function and educational lessons to children about how to overcome inner conflicts and deal with anxieties. Bettelheim argued for the importance of the violent aspects of fairy tales because they give cathartic expression to our dark side and they permit the child a safe opportunity to fit 'unconscious content into conscious fantasies, which then enable him [sic] to deal with that content' (1991 [1976]: 7). Though Bettelheim's methodology and work is now much criticized, his view of fairy tales is still widely cited and has proved influential on research into the positive uses of violent fantasy, including the use of fantasy violence in play. In 2002, 33 media scholars joined in a court brief to counter simplistic assumptions about effects, and they suggest that fantasy violence of the type found in many films, video games and superhero comics is understood and used by children as fantasy and therefore should not be censored (see The St Louis Court Brief 2003 [2002]).

Though film audiences can and do use superhero characters and comic book fantasy violence in many different ways, the fact remains that Hollywood uses them principally for selling. In the case of *The Dark Knight*, an elaborate viral marketing campaign generated buzz about the film and more specifically the Joker character, and tie-in merchandise such as video games, clothing and toys (many of which were marketed at young children) went on sale in stores prior to the cinema release date. In an era when blockbuster fantasy brands like Batman are doing big business for media conglomerates it seems difficult (perhaps impossible) to attempt to reconcile every classification decision with the demands of entertainment, commercial needs, public opinion and our view of audiences, and debates about the category of fantasy violence are likely to continue for a long time to come.

FANTASY STORYTELLING

Despite the importance of violence to much traditional oral and literary folk and fairy storytelling, thanks mainly to Disney, the dominant tendency for most popular fairy tale fantasy films has been to sanitize and repackage them, strongly emphasizing the 'happily ever after'. These days the mention of fairy tale is likely to bring to mind the now classic and highly commercial 'Disneyfied' versions with which most of us become familiar (from the Disney Channel, DVD films and other media), the anthropomorphized animal characters who populate the animated films, theme parks and stores where they appear on and as merchandise, and the conservative family-friendly ideological values that the Disney brand represents. As a result critical scholarship on Disney is wide-ranging in its attention to aspects of the phenomenon, including history, globalization, marketing, story, aesthetics and politics. In *Understanding Disney: The Manufacture of Fantasy* (2001) Janet Wasko gives a comprehensive overview of the main debates in Disney studies to date, and the impact on popular culture. She concludes that crucial to understanding the worldwide success of Disney is brand power and recognition: 'The Disney Company has grown and expanded by vigilantly controlling its products, characters and images and developing its reputation as a company that produces positive, wholesome, family and children's entertainment' (Wasko 2001: 222).

It is widely recognized that over the years Disney has had a significant influence on culture, the Hollywood film industry, animation and on storytelling. In the discipline of fairy tale studies much work is done on how the Disney formula changes and adapts fairy tales and to what effect. Jack Zipes (e.g. 1994, 2002) writes a great deal about the ways in which the culture industry in general, and Disney in particular, exploits the fairy tale for the purposes of commercial entertainment. According to Zipes, beginning in the 1920s and 1930s Disney 'cast a spell on the fairy tale, and it has been held captive ever since' (1994: 72). For Zipes and many other critics the spell that Disney cast over the fairy tale is actually more of an evil curse. Criticisms of Disney films include the representation of gender and sexual stereotypes, racism and the hegemonic process of American cultural imperialism (e.g. Bell *et al.* 1995). Zipes therefore accuses Walt Disney of violating the genre of fairy tale:

> Instead of using technology to enhance the communal aspects of narrative and bring about major changes in viewing stories to stir and animate viewers, he employed animators and technology to stop thinking about change, to return to his films, and to long nostalgically for neatly ordered patriarchal realms.
>
> (Zipes 1994: 95)

Elsewhere, though, Zipes demonstrates that there are films which seek to break the magic spell (or curse) of the Disney Corporation. In a recently revised edition of the aptly titled *Breaking the Magic Spell*, Zipes calls attention to the way that the animated film version from DreamWorks (2001) of William Steig's 1990 children's book *Shrek* challenges some accepted standards and 'goes beyond the Disney animated fairy-tale films' (2002: 230). He says that 'Radical in plot, radical in technique, *Shrek* is an unusual film because it opens up questions about the conflict within the culture industry with regard to who is going to control the realm of animation and amusement for the young' (Zipes 2002: 228).

Perhaps what is most interesting about the film version of *Shrek* is the way that it exposes, and to an extent undermines, those codes and conventions that govern fairy tale storytelling in the Disney tradition and define our expectations about the genre. In fact, *Shrek* takes a self-conscious approach to storytelling right from the very start, when the classic opening signalled by an illustrated storybook and a 'Once upon a time' fairy tale is abruptly ended when the narrator Shrek unexpectedly breaks off to comment 'Like that's ever gonna happen', and then recycles a page for use in his ogre outhouse. Like the rest of the film, this scene is hardly subtle in tone or message to the viewer: it cues us to the fact that *Shrek* is an irreverent take on the fairy tale and much of the humour comes from reading the various parodic intertextual strategies the filmmakers employ. In addition to contemporary pop culture references (including many fantasy films) *Shrek* draws from well-known fairy tale elements to ironize rather than idealize them. Thus classic stock characters such as the ugly ogre, the beautiful princess and the fierce dragon, and storytelling clichés like the quest, rescue, curse and romance, are present but roles are reversed, conventions undercut and appearances often deceptive.

For example, in the same way that our expectation of a traditional fairy tale story is subverted by the opening prologue, we soon find that Princess Fiona is not the stereotypical helpless maiden we think. Though, in line with fairy tale conventions, the story has Fiona trapped in a castle tower passively waiting to get rescued by a handsome (and romantic) prince, not only is she actually set free by an ugly (and rude) ogre, but it also turns out she is clever (impolite) and something of an action heroine, as evidenced by the scene where she uses *The Matrix*-style (1999) kung fu skills to fight Robin Hood and his Merry Men. When Shrek fails to look, behave or respond like a typical fairy tale hero, Fiona realizes that he is not the Prince Charming she had been led to expect (by fairy tales), and she stops playing the traditional role of the damsel in distress too. Indeed, the characters in *Shrek* are generally just as knowing as the audience about what is and what is not supposed to happen in a classic fairy tale and this is exploited to comic effect.

Shrek also includes a cast of familiar fairy tale characters, such as the Three Little Pigs, the Gingerbread Man and the Big Bad Wolf. But taken out of their traditional storybook settings and put on screen these characters literally become exiles in Shrek's swamp and they effectively take refuge in his tale, having been banished from the realm of Duloc by the evil Lord Farquaad. In contrast to the general messages of tolerance and understanding of difference that comes out of Shrek's quest to get his swamp back (which sets in motion his inner search for self-acceptance) is the oppressive totalitarianism of Farquaad's aim to establish absolute control over Duloc. The despotic (and vertically-challenged) ruler has ordered a kind of ethnic cleansing of fairy tale characters from his kingdom, because to Farquaad they are 'fairy tale trash, poisoning my perfect world'. It is no secret that Farquaad and Duloc operate as part of Shrek's critique of the Disney empire which, according to Zipes, also 'wants the world cleaned up' (1994: 92, emphasis in original). Zipes sees Duloc as 'a sanitized Disney world in perfect symmetry' (2002: 229), a remark which refers to the strong resemblance between Duloc and Disneyland no doubt apparent to most viewers. In the DVD commentary the filmmakers similarly describe Duloc as a 'fascist theme park', represented by the queue and turnstile system, box office, souvenir shop and Main Street USA-type pristine street that Shrek and Donkey find when they visit Farquaad. It has also been said that Farquaad was partly based on then head of the Disney Corporation Michael Eisner due to the animosity Shrek's co-producer and DreamWorks co-founder Jeffrey Katzenberg felt towards his former employer. In many ways it seems like DreamWorks itself may have been founded to rival Disney's dominance over animation and what is known as the Disney storytelling formula.

Shrek's critique of Disney is made further apparent by the parodying of Disney fairy tale characters and scenes from film classics including Snow White and the Seven Dwarfs (1937), Pinocchio (1940), Sleeping Beauty (1958) and Beauty and the Beast (1991). Clear visual references prompt the viewer to recall these much-loved Disney productions, but the words and actions of the characters themselves are changed and scenes given a different twist. Hence Gepetto is seen selling Pinocchio to Farquaad's men during the amnesty that is part of the villain's fairy tale cleansing towards the start of the film; Shrek bellows at the seven dwarfs 'Dead broad off the table!' when they bring Snow White in her glass coffin to his cottage having just been resettled to his swamp (Figure 4.5); and in a sequence that satirizes Disney-style musical numbers, when Fiona sings with a bird in the forest her pitch gets so high that the

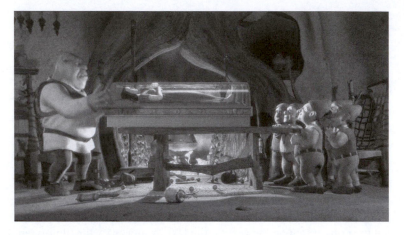

Figure 4.5   'Dead broad off the table!' *Shrek* spoofs familiar Disney fairy tale characters and storytelling

bird finally explodes in a puff of feathers leaving behind its eggs (seemingly unaffected by the bird's death Fiona cooks the eggs for Shrek and Donkey at breakfast).

While *Shrek* has a happy ending, there is another subversion of a traditional fairy tale storyline, especially the 'Beauty and the Beast' story (to which *Shrek* is often compared) and specifically the Disney version. At the film's finale is a scene that spoofs the Beast's transformation at the conclusion of Disney's *Beauty and the Beast*, when the enchantment is lifted and the Beast magically returns to his human form. This transformation is reversed in *Shrek*, with Fiona becoming an ogress rather than the ogre Shrek becoming a handsome prince. It follows that in the final moments of the film, as Shrek and Fiona are married and ride off together into the sunset and the storybook closes, we learn that 'They lived ugly ever after' in a suitably ironic variation on the classic fairy tale ending. For Zipes what is especially important about *Shrek* is that, in addition to undercutting conventional notions of beauty, at the end of this morally significant story, 'The ogre and his wife will continue to frighten people, but they will be happy to do so in the name of relative morality that questions the bias of conventionality associated with evil' (2002: 228). And in his view:

> One of the 'moral' questions that *Shrek* raises is: must we continue to stuff the brains of our children with sentimental stereotyped films produced by the Disney corporation which, for over sixty-five years, has dominated animation and mass-mediated fairy tales?
>
> (Zipes 2002: 229–30)

Zipes is not alone in welcoming *Shrek* as a positive example of how the fairy tale is revised and redefined in self-reflexive and 'compelling' (anti-Disney) ways, and the subversive potential that the fairy tale film might still offer us in the contemporary world (2007: 30). At the time of the cinema release the media were generally approving of *Shrek*'s playful postmodern approach to the fairy tale story, and scholars note that the film addresses some issues of representation, particularly the gender codes underlying the narrative strategies of traditional tales (e.g. Fowkes 2010: 119–22).

At the same time however it must be acknowledged that *Shrek* is not without its limitations and others have criticized the fact that the film, and even more so the sequels that follow, not only comment on commodification and consumerism, but also engage in these practices which are typical of the culture industry. On the one hand the next three *Shrek* films continue to use contemporary cultural references and attitudes to parody the traditional fairy tale, and Shrek and Fiona must deal with problems that follow happy ever afters: from Shrek's struggle to gain acceptance from Fiona's royal parents and the scheming Fairy Godmother's attempts to break up the newlyweds in *Shrek 2* (2004); to his fears about parental and royal responsibility and the attack of the feminist princesses in *Shrek The Third* (2007), and the alternate fairy tale reality scenario of *Shrek Forever After* (2010) that finally (by all accounts) brings the ogre's tale to an end. On the other hand, these animated films form part of what has arguably become just another franchise (including a 4D theme park ride, *Shrek the Musical* live stage production, video games, toys, fast food tie-ins, spin-off television specials and a film about Puss in Boots reportedly scheduled for release in 2011), and DreamWorks's efforts to merchandise the multi-billion dollar Shrek brand is similar to the Disney model. (For an interesting discussion of the potentially subversive themes in *Shrek* and *Shrek 2* in the commercial context of the culture industry, see Crandall 2006.)

Other recent animated and live-action fantasy films also use comedy to deconstruct traditional fairy tale storytelling and motifs. Some examples include *The Brothers Grimm* (2005), *Hoodwinked!* (2005), *Happily N'Ever After* (2007) and *Stardust* (2007). And not wanting to be outdone by the *Shrek* phenomenon, in 2007 Disney released *Enchanted*, a film which starts as a classic 2D animated fairy tale set in the fantasy land of Andalasia, and then shifts to live-action and the 'realistic' world of modern-day New York. Similar to *Shrek*, *Enchanted* includes many references to past Disney works and the film is advertised (on the DVD box) as 'A New Disney Classic With a Twist'. Most critics agree though that the 'twist' in this instance is seriously limited, not least because parody soon yields to homage and, in the words of Cristina Bacchilega and John Rieder, 'The film's insistent clash of worlds and genres merely consolidates a normative project that exploitatively sells a watered-down representation of feminism [and Disney's lucrative "Princess" franchise]' (2010: 30). Nevertheless such fairy tale films perhaps demonstrate how, in the twenty-first century, fantasy storytelling will find ways to carry on evolving.

FANTASY TIME

Another direction that storytelling in fantasy film takes is towards tales about time travel, which is surely one of our most compelling fantasies. Is there anyone who would refuse the chance to witness firsthand what human beings will be like in two thousand years, or the possibility of actually being there to see spectacular moments of history unfold? And who would refuse the opportunity to return to a crucial moment in the past and change the course of history for the better? Richard Matthews calls time travel an 'archetypal impulse . . . inextricably woven into the inspiration and essence of modern fantasy', at the heart of which is the 'impulse to explore and recover the past' (2002: 26).

All film can make time slow, stop, stretch, and reverse, leap ahead and back, shrink, speed up, be elided, or repeated; film is able to present time in any order, and reverse the future-directed flow of cause and effect. Film time may revisit historical (or mythical) periods, travel to the future, (re)create and bring together historical and present time, future and present time, or even historical, present, and future time (see Furby 2005: 18–19). Such films can offer us the fantasy of freedom of movement in time. In the real world we have very limited potential for time travel. We cannot move backwards to a period before our birth, nor forwards to a time after our death, and the time in-between these moments must be lived in sequential order at the rate of one second per second; we cannot change the speed of the clock. In a very real sense the past can only be accessed through memory, and we cannot experience the future, only anticipate it. As fantasy film viewers though, we can travel into the past or to the future, and enjoy a fantasy of freedom from our real world restrictions of movement in time.

Time-based fantasy film includes body swap fantasy, fantasies of time behaving strangely, and time travel. The early 1980s, for instance, saw a number of body-swap films (e.g. *Like Father, Like Son*, 1987; *Big*, 1988; and *Vice-Versa*, 1988). The category of time behaving strangely includes time slip stories where characters inexplicably find that they have shifted in time (e.g. *Premonition*, 2007), and time loop stories where characters become trapped in a pattern of repeated time without any explanation, like *Groundhog Day* (1993) and *Lola Rennt/Run, Lola, Run* (1998). Many time travel films belong resolutely to the science fiction genre because their plots revolve around the science, technology, paradoxes or rules of time travel (e.g. *Time Cop*, 1984; *Primer*, 2004). Other time travel films where the mechanism of time travel is left mysteriously unexplored can clearly be claimed for the fantasy genre, such as *Time Bandits* (1981), *Peggy Sue Got Married* (1986), and *The Time Traveler's Wife* (2009). This leaves a number of time travel films that sit on the boundary between fantasy and science fiction. In these films there may be a vaguely science-based explanation for the time travel and some discussion of time paradoxes, but the emphasis is on the desires, aspirations, fantasies and fears of the character(s). Examples of this type include *Twelve Monkeys* (1995), and *Back to the Future* (1985), which focus on fantasies of redemption and rescue.

The central, structuring motif which drives the plot of *Back to the Future* is that events in the past can be changed to ensure a successful life for Marty McFly and his family in the present. However, when Marty first arrives in 1955 from 1985, he inadvertently alters past events, the result of which is a temporal paradox: he encounters the girl originally destined to become his mother and, in a plotline that more than hints at incest and Oedipal phantasy, prevents the initial meeting between her and his future father (see Gordon 2004). A result of his interaction with his mother is that he jeopardizes his own chances of being born (see Fhlainn 2010 for a collection of essays on the Back to the Future film trilogy). Of course the paradox is that if he does not exist in the future of this new timeline, then he cannot travel back in time to alter his own destiny. In order to resolve the paradox he must make things happen as they did in the original timeline so that he can (still) be born. In resolving the paradox Marty is in effect saving his own life (and also, as Constance Penley (1996) contends, playing out a Freudian primal scene fantasy of being instrumental in his own conception).

Back to the Future involves Marty saving himself, but many past-directed time travel films are concerned with rescuing others. For example, in Timescape (1992), Ben Wilson is able to bring back his dead daughter and wife by using time travel technology brought to his time from the future by visiting temporal tourists. And in Timecop Max Walker unravels a complex sequence of events in spacetime to rescue his dead wife and their unborn child, whilst in Frequency (2000) John Sullivan makes use of a temporary temporal anomaly to recover his dead father. In other films like The Terminator (1984), La Jetée (1962), and Twelve Monkeys the whole of humanity is the object of rescue.

One of Twelve Monkeys's central themes is that the past is never dead and laid to rest, but, like memory and experience buried in the human psyche, continually exerts a pressure and an influence on the present. Indeed, time is presented as a continuous loop, and the chief protagonist, James Cole, is caught up, like a hamster in a wheel, in a temporal pattern from which he is unable to escape. The opening shot of the film is of a pair of eyes. The final shot is of the same pair of eyes, belonging, as is evident by this point in the film, to Cole as an eight-year-old child who has just witnessed the fatal shooting of a man at an airport. The amount of chronological time that passes between these two images is just a few minutes, but the film's plot follows the adult Cole's journey in time as he is sent backwards and forwards between 2035 and 1990 and 1996 (with a brief accidental diversion to 1917), only to return to the airport to fulfil his destiny as the man his eight-year-old self saw being shot (see Wood 2002: 48–78).

We are first introduced to the adult Cole in his 2035 reality, an Orwellian dystopia where he is imprisoned for crimes against authority. In this reality attention is focused on the year of 1996, when the world's population was devastated by a viral plague, forcing the one per cent who survived to seek refuge underground. Cole is 'volunteered' to time travel to before the virus was released, in order to track down a sample of the pure virus so that the future population might find a cure and be able to return to the surface of the Earth. On one level this is a detective adventure story which charts his difficult navigation of the vicissitudes of time travel whilst trying to solve the mystery of the viral perpetrator. On another level Twelve Monkeys explores Cole's troubled internal mental landscape. In fact, an alternative reading of the film is that he is mentally divergent and simply hallucinating his time travel experiences, which invokes Tzvetan Todorov's (1977) notion of the hesitation of the fantastic between two possible explanations of events that influence how we view him: either he is mad or a time-traveller.

Patricia Pisters notes the popularity of the themes of 'time and memory in relation to subjectivity and selfhood' in contemporary cinema (2003: 39), and these themes are brought together in Cole's story to define him. He has a memory, which repeatedly returns to him as dream fragments, in which he witnesses the death referred to above. Witnessing the death could be read as a Lacanian mirror stage moment (Lacan 2001) as it sets in motion Cole's development into the rebellious character who ends up imprisoned and as a result is forced to return to the past to meet his fate, because as the loop of time tightens we realize that the death he remembers is actually his own. For Cole, the death scene, and what happens afterwards, describes a complete circle and though he is successful in solving the mystery of the virus's origins, the film entraps him in a claustrophobic cycle of time from which there is no escape.

In Twelve Monkeys there is a tension between freedom of action, and determinism which allows for little freedom of choice (see Lucas 2009: 533–40). Though the fantasy of roaming around in time might suggest a great freedom, going backwards in time to complete a cycle of events that have already occurred effectively removes any sense of freedom from the time-traveller. This irony is seen in the logo of the monkeys formed in a circle (Figure 4.6), with one (presumably Cole) breaking free (see Devlin 2008). The film sets Cole up as a renegade character who rebels against society, but his rebellion simply results in his imprisonment and places him at the mercy of the scientists who send him back in time to his inevitable death, at which moment he recognizes that he is already dead, and so he dies again. In this way, Twelve Monkeys suggests a dark, pessimistic version of time travel where dying once means becoming locked into a pattern and being fated to die over and over again.

Prince of Persia: The Sands of Time (2010) is a film that gives a different take on the notion of destiny. This is a fantasy which transports us back to a mythical time, and it is also a fantasy about the manipulation of time. The story has the structure and character types of a traditional folktale. Dastan is of common birth, but noble of heart and spirit, an orphan street boy, adopted by King Sharaman, who becomes a Prince of the enormously powerful Persian Empire. As in many traditional stories, nobility of birth, and a heroic bloodline, is not necessarily the only prophetic marker of a splendid destiny; nobility of heart and spirit also count. In his adoptive family he is now the youngest of three brothers, a common trope in myth, tale and legend, and he even bears an archetypal name, as Dastan is Persian for 'hero'. Furthermore there is a good king, who has an evil and ambitious brother, and of course there is a beautiful princess to provide the hero with a prize to mark his ultimate triumph.

The film is adapted from the video game of the same name, and employs gaming logic such as allowing the characters/players a chance to redo the action from cycle to cycle/level to level (literally to re-play time), by means of a magical dagger. Also associated with the video game is the markedly fast-paced action and skilled movement through space achieved by the gaming characters, and by characters in the film, particularly Dastan. When we first meet him, he is a child who evades his pursuers by leaping across the rooftops, and when we next meet him as an adult his athleticism provides the film with a key spectacle (Figure 4.7). Dastan's ability to climb vertical planes and leap remarkable distances and from impressive heights appears to defy the laws of gravity (an effect achieved using the real world technique of Parkour).

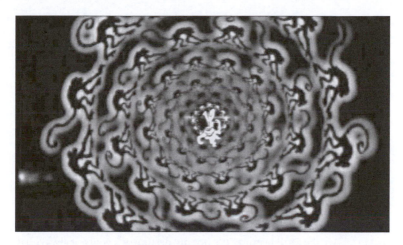

Figure 4.6　Monkeys trapped in a time loop in *Twelve Monkeys*

Figure 4.7　Dastan demonstrates spectacular freedom in space in *Prince of Persia: The Sands of Time*

In addition to this spectacular mastery of space, Dastan gains freedom of movement in time when he gets control of the mystical dagger fashioned with a glass phial to hold special sand in the handle. In a moment of exposition Dastan tells us that:

> Releasing the sand turns back time, and only the holder of the dagger is aware of what's happened. He can go back and alter events, change

time, and no-one knows but him . . . With it he could change the course of a critical moment in battle, he could foresee the blade of a rival.

Dastan's uncle, Nizam, wants to acquire the dagger and, by plunging it into a 'container holding the fabled Sands of Time . . . corrupt history . . . turn back time and make himself king', and it is Dastan's destiny to prevent this from happening.

Prince of Persia opens with a statement that 'It is said that some lives are linked across time, connected by an ancient calling that echoes through the ages . . . destiny', and there is much further talk of Dastan's destiny throughout the film. For example, Dastan's adoptive father reminds him that he recognized the poor street orphan was destined for greatness. And Princess Tamina tells Dastan to save the Earth because 'It's not my destiny, it's yours. It always has been'. The film's temporal logic thus allows for free will in an open future, but this is against a deterministic, closed timescape where future actions were already set long ago. The film nevertheless manages to invoke a sense of triumphant proactivity as Dastan (the spectator's on-screen surrogate) wins through, by virtue of his physical strength, bravery, prowess, strength of character and nobility, to achieve actual and moral supremacy over his enemies.

Towards the end of the film, in order for Dastan to prove to his brother Tus that he is innocent of killing their father, he thrusts the dagger into his own heart, and dies. As Dastan lies dead, Tus uses the dagger to bring him back to life. Like Cole in Twelve Monkeys Dastan dies, but unlike Cole he is able to defeat death and return (like the video game player), to restart the action, this time with additional knowledge and refined skills, with more than a measure of control over his own fate. Tellingly, in the climactic scene, when Nizam has jeopardized the whole world by plunging the mystical dagger into the Sandglass of the Gods, Dastan is able to control and stem the flow of time at exactly the right moment to save the city and undo the damage that been done. He thereby redeems all the lost lives (including those of King Sharaman, Tus, and Tamina). In doing so he paradoxically controls destiny, which is the idea of an inescapable future, and this is notable and ironic in a film about successfully undoing the past. In *Prince of Persia* Dastan is successful, unlike Cole in *Twelve Monkeys*, in redeeming the past, rescuing his own present and guaranteeing himself a happy future. Time and destiny are on his side. These elements, time and destiny, represent two of the many pillars that form the deepest foundations of fantasy in storytelling and in film.

FILMOGRAPHY

The list below contains details (sourced from *Film Index International*) of the fantasy films we mention in this book. We have opted to include some films that might be considered to occupy the boundaries or 'water margins' (Clute and Grant 1997: 997, and see our Chapter 1) of fantasy and other related film movements and genres, though our central focus on the mainstream means that most come out of Hollywood. Certainly, our fantasy filmography is indicative rather than comprehensive and can be used as a starting point for further viewing and research.

2001: A Space Odyssey (Stanley Kubrick, 1968, USA)

10,000 B.C. (Roland Emmerich, 2008, USA/South Africa)

The 7th Voyage of Sinbad (Nathan Juran, 1958, USA)

The Absent Minded Professor (Robert Stevenson, 1961, USA)

The Adventures of Robin Hood (Michael Curtiz/William Keighley, 1938, USA)

L'Âge D'Or (Luis Buñuel, 1930, France/Spain)

Ali Baba et les Quarante Voleurs/Ali Baba and the Forty Thieves (Ferdinand Zecca, 1902, France)

Alice in Wonderland (Cecil B. Hepworth/Percy Stow, 1903, UK)

Alice in Wonderland (Tim Burton, 2010, USA)

Antz (Eric Darnell/Tim Johnson, 1998, USA)

Avatar (James Cameron, 2009, USA/UK)

Back to the Future (Robert Zemeckis, 1985, USA)

Batman (Tim Burton, 1989, USA/UK)

Batman Returns (Tim Burton, 1992, USA)

Batman Begins (Christopher Nolan, 2005, USA/UK)

The Beast From 2,000 Fathoms (Eugène Lourié, 1953, USA)

The Beastmaster (Don Coscarelli, 1982, USA/Germany)

Beauty and the Beast (Gary Trousdale/Kirk Wise, 1991, USA)

La Belle et la Bête/Beauty and the Beast (Jean Cocteau, 1946, France)

Beowulf (Robert Zemeckis, 2007, USA)

Big (Penny Marshall, 1988, USA)

Bill and Ted's Excellent Adventure (Stephen Herek, 1988, USA)

The Brothers Grimm (Terry Gilliam, 2005, USA/Czech Republic)

Cabin in the Sky (Vincente Minnelli, 1943, USA)

Das Cabinet des Dr Caligari /The Cabinet of Dr Caligari (Robert Wiene, 1920, Germany)

Cendrillon/Cinderella (Georges Méliès, 1899, France)

Charlie and the Chocolate Factory (Tim Burton, 2005, USA/UK/Australia)

Un Chien Andalou/An Andalusian Dog (Luis Buñuel, 1928, France)

The Chronicles of Narnia: The Lion, the Witch and the Wardrobe (Andrew Adamson, 2005, USA)

The Chronicles of Narnia: Prince Caspian (Andrew Adamson, 2008, USA)

The Chronicles of Narnia: The Voyage of the Dawn Treader (Michael Apted, 2010, USA)

Cinderella (Wilfred Jackson/Clyde Geronimi/Hamilton Luske, 1949, USA)

Clash of the Titans (Desmond Davis, 1981, USA/UK)

Clash of the Titans (Louis Leterrier, 2010, USA)

The Company of Wolves (Neil Jordan, 1984, UK)

Conan the Barbarian (John Milius, 1982, USA)

Conan the Destroyer (Richard Fleischer, 1984, USA)

The Dark Crystal (Frank Oz/Jim Henson, 1982, USA/UK)

The Dark Knight (Christopher Nolan, 2008, USA/UK)

The Devil and Daniel Webster/All That Money Can Buy (Wilhelm Dieterle, 1941, USA)

Dragonheart (Rob Cohen, 1996, USA)

Dragonslayer (Matthew Robbins, 1981, USA)

The Dream of a Rarebit Fiend (Wallace McCutcheon/Edwin S. Porter, 1906, USA)

Edward Scissorhands (Tim Burton, 1990, USA)

The Empire Strikes Back (Irvin Kershner, 1980, USA)

Enchanted (Kevin Lima, 2007, USA)

The Enchanted Cottage (John Cromwell, 1945, USA)

E.T.: The Extra-Terrestrial (Steven Spielberg, 1982, USA)

Excalibur (John Boorman, 1981, USA)

Fantasmagorie (Émile Cohl, 1908, France)

Faust (F.W. Murnau, 1926, Germany)

Final Fantasy: The Spirits Within (Hironobu Sakaguchi, 2001, USA)

First Knight (Jerry Zucker, 1995, USA)

Frequency (Gregory Hoblit, 2000, USA)

Gertie the Dinosaur (Winsor McCay, 1914, USA)

Ghost (Jerry Zucker, 1990, USA)

The Ghost and Mrs Muir (Joseph L. Mankiewicz, 1947, USA)

The Golden Compass (Chris Weitz, 2007, USA/UK)

The Golden Voyage of Sinbad (Gordon Hessler, 1973, USA)

Groundhog Day (Harold Ramis, 1993, USA)

Gulliver's Travels (Dave Fleischer, 1939, USA)

A Guy Named Joe (Victor Fleming, 1944, USA)

Les Hallucinations du Baron de Munchausen/Baron Munchausen's Dream (Georges Méliès, 1911, France)

Happily N'Ever After (Paul J. Bolger, 2007, USA/Germany)

Harry Potter and the Chamber of Secrets (Chris Columbus, 2002, USA/UK/Germany)

Harry Potter and the Deathly Hallows: Part 1 (David Yates, 2010, USA/UK)

Harry Potter and the Goblet of Fire (Mike Newell, 2005, USA/UK)

Harry Potter and the Half-Blood Prince (David Yates, 2009, USA/UK)

Harry Potter and the Order of the Phoenix (David Yates, 2007, USA/UK)

Harry Potter and the Philosopher's Stone (Chris Columbus, 2001, USA/UK)

Harry Potter and the Prisoner of Azkaban (Alfonso Cuarón, 2004, USA/UK)

Hauru no ugoku shiro/Howl's Moving Castle (Hayao Miyazaki, 2004, Japan)

Hawk the Slayer (Terry Marcel, 1980, UK)

Hellboy (Guillermo del Toro, 2004, USA)

Hellboy II: The Golden Army (Guillermo del Toro, 2008, USA/Germany)

Here Comes Mr Jordan (Alexander Hall, 1941, USA)

Der Himmel über Berlin/Wings of Desire (Wim Wenders, 1987, West Germany/France)

L'Homme à la Tête de Caoutchouc/The Man with the Rubber Head (Georges Méliès, 1902, France)

Hoodwinked! (Cory Edwards, 2005, USA)

How to Train Your Dragon (Chris Sanders, 2010, USA)

Indiana Jones and the Kingdom of the Crystal Skull (Steven Spielberg, 2008, USA)

Indiana Jones and the Last Crusade (Steven Spielberg, 1989, USA)

Indiana Jones and the Temple of Doom (Steven Spielberg, 1984, USA)

It's a Wonderful Life (Frank Capra, 1947, USA)

Jason and the Argonauts (Don Chaffey, 1963, USA/UK)

Journey to the Center of the Earth (Henry Levin, 1959, USA)

Journey to the Center of the Earth (Eric Brevig, 2008, USA)

The Jungle Book (Wolfgang Reitherman, 1967, USA)

Jurassic Park (Steven Spielberg, 1993, USA)

King Kong (Merian C. Cooper/Ernest B. Schoedsack, 1933, USA)

King Kong (Peter Jackson, 2005, USA/Germany/New Zealand)

A Knight's Tale (Brian Helgeland, 2001, USA)

Krull (Peter Yates, 1983, UK)

El laberinto del fauno/Pan's Labyrinth (Guillermo del Toro, 2006, Spain/Mexico/USA)

Labyrinth (Jim Henson, 1986, UK)

Lara Croft: Tomb Raider (Simon West, 2001, USA/Germany/UK/Japan)

Legend (Ridley Scott, 1985, USA)

Lekce Faust/Faust (Jan Švankmajer, 1994, Czech Republic/France/UK/Germany)

Like Father, Like Son (Rod Daniel, 1987, USA)

The Little Mermaid (John Musker/Ron Clements, 1989, USA)

Lola Rennt/Run, Lola, Run (Tom Tykwer, 1998, Germany)

The Lord of the Rings (Ralph Bakshi, 1978, USA)

The Lord of the Rings: The Fellowship of the Ring (Peter Jackson, 2001, USA/New Zealand)

The Lord of the Rings: Return of the King (Peter Jackson, 2003, USA/New Zealand/Germany)

The Lord of the Rings: The Two Towers (Peter Jackson, 2002, USA/New Zealand/Germany)

Lost Horizon (Frank Capra, 1937, USA)

The Lost World (Harry O. Hoyt, 1925, USA)

A Midsummer Night's Dream (Michael Hoffman, 1999, USA/Germany)

The Magic Sword (Walter R. Booth, 1901, UK)

Mary Poppins (Robert Stevenson, 1964, USA)

A Matter of Life and Death (Michael Powell and Emeric Pressburger, 1946, UK)

Mononoke-hime/Princess Mononoke (Hayao Miyazaki, 1997, Japan)

Der Müd Tod/Destiny (Fritz Lang, 1921, Germany)

Mulholland Drive (David Lynch, 2001, USA/France)

Münchhausen (Josef von Baky, 1943, Germany)

Mysterious Island (Cy Endfield, 1961, USA/UK)

Neco z Alenky/Alice (Jan Švankmajer, 1988, Switzerland/UK/West Germany)

The NeverEnding Story (Wolfgang Petersen, 1984, Germany)

Die Nibelungen 1 Teil: Siegfried/The Nibelungen Part 1: Siegfried (Fritz Lang, 1924, Germany)

Die Nibelungen 2 Teil: Kriemhilds Rache/The Nibelungen Part 2: Kriemhild's Revenge (Fritz Lang, 1924, Germany)

The Nightmare Before Christmas (Henry Selick, 1993; 3D 2006, USA)

Orphée/Orpheus (Jean Cocteau, 1950, France)

Otesánek/Little Otik (Jan Švankmajer, 2000, Czech Republic/UK/Japan)

Peggy Sue Got Married (Francis Ford Coppola, 1986, USA)

Percy Jackson and the Olympians: The Lightning Thief (Chris Columbus, 2010, USA/Australia/UK)

Le Petite Chaperon Rouge/Little Red Riding Hood (Georges Méliès, 1901, France)

Pinocchio (Ben Sharpsteen/Hamilton Luske, 1940, USA)

Pirates of the Caribbean: At World's End (Gore Verbinski, 2007, USA)

Pirates of the Caribbean: The Curse of the Black Pearl (Gore Verbinski, 2003, USA)

Pirates of the Caribbean: Dead Man's Chest (Gore Verbinski, 2006, USA)

Pleasantville (Gary Ross, 1998, USA)

The Polar Express (Robert Zemeckis, 2004, USA)

Poslední trik pana Schwarcewalldea a pana Edgara/The Last Trick (Jan Švankmajer, 1964, Czechoslovakia)

Practical Magic (Griffin Dunne, 1998, USA/Australia)

Premonition (Mennan Yapo, 2007, USA/UK)

Prince of Persia: The Sands of Time (Mike Newell, 2010, USA)

Raiders of the Lost Ark (Steven Spielberg, 1981, USA)

Der Rattenfänger von Hameln / The Pied Piper of Hamelin (Paul Wegener, 1918, Germany)

Red Sonja (Richard Fleischer, 1985, USA)

Return of the Jedi (Richard Marquand, 1983, USA)

Robin Hood: Prince of Thieves (Kevin Reynolds, 1991, USA)

Sen to Chihiro no kamikakushi / Spirited Away (Hayao Miyazaki, 2001, Japan)

Shrek (Andrew Adamson/Vicky Jenson, 2001, USA)

Shrek 2 (Andrew Adamson/Kelly Asbury/Conrad Vernon, 2004, USA)

Shrek Forever After (Mike Mitchell, 2010, USA)

Shrek The Third (Chris Miller, 2007, USA)

Sinbad and the Eye of the Tiger (Sam Wanamaker, 1977, USA)

Sleeping Beauty (Clyde Geronimi, 1958, USA)

Sleepy Hollow (Tim Burton, 1999, USA/Germany)

Snow White and the Seven Dwarfs (David Hand, 1937, USA)

Spider-Man (Sam Raimi, 2002, USA)

Spider-Man 2 (Sam Raimi, 2004, USA)

Spider-Man 3 (Sam Raimi, 2007, USA)

The Spirit (Frank Miller, 2008, USA)

Stardust (Matthew Vaughn, 2007, USA/UK)

Star Wars (George Lucas, 1977, USA)

Star Wars Episode I: The Phantom Menace (George Lucas, 1999, USA)

Star Wars Episode II: Attack of the Clones (George Lucas, 2002, USA)

Star Wars Episode III: Revenge of the Sith (George Lucas, 2005, USA)

Superman (Richard Donner, 1978, USA/Switzerland/UK/Panama)

The Sword and the Sorcerer (Albert Pyun, 1982, USA)

The Sword in the Stone (Wolfgang Reitherman, 1963, USA)

Sword of the Valiant: The Legend of Gawain and the Green Knight (Stephen Weeks, 1984, UK)

The Tempest (Julie Taymor, 2011, USA)

The Thief of Bagdad (Raoul Walsh, 1924, USA)

The Thief of Bagdad (Ludwig Berger/Michael Powell/Tim Whelhan, 1940, UK)

Time Bandits (Terry Gilliam, 1981, UK)

Timescape (David N. Twohy, 1992, USA)

The Time Traveler's Wife (Robert Schwentke, 2009, USA)

Topper (Norman Z. McLeod, 1937, USA)

Toy Story (John Lasseter, 1995; 3D 2009, USA)

Tron (Steven Lisberger, 1982, USA)

Troy (Wolfgang Petersen, 2004, USA/UK/Malta)

Twelve Monkeys (Terry Gilliam, 1995, USA)

Twilight (Catherine Hardwicke, 2008, USA)

The Twilight Saga: Eclipse (David Slade, 2010, USA)

The Twilight Saga: New Moon (Chris Weitz, 2009, USA)

Up (Robert Docter/Bob Petersen, 2009, USA)

Vice-Versa (Brian Gilbert, 1988, USA)

Le Voyage dans le Lune/A Trip to the Moon (Georges Méliès, 1902, France)

What Lies Beneath (Robert Zemeckis, 2000, USA)

Who Framed Roger Rabbit? (Robert Zemeckis, 1988, USA)

Willow (Ron Howard, 1988, USA)

The Wizard of Oz (Victor Fleming, 1939, USA)

The Wonderful World of the Brothers Grimm (Henry Levin/George Pal, 1962, USA)

Zvahlav aneb Saticky Slameného Huberta/Jabberwocky (Jan Švankmajer, 1971, Czechoslovakia)

BIBLIOGRAPHY

Allen, M. (1998) 'From Bwana Devil to Batman Forever: Technology in Contemporary Hollywood Cinema', in S. Neale and M. Smith (eds) *Contemporary Hollywood Cinema*, London: Routledge.

—— (2003) *Contemporary US Cinema*, Harlow: Longman.

Altman, R. (2004) *Silent Film Sound*, New York: Columbia University Press.

Aristotle (2008) *Poetics*, trans. S.H. Butcher, New York: Cosimo.

Attebery, B. (1992) *Strategies of Fantasy*, Bloomington and Indianapolis: Indiana University Press.

Bacchilega, C. (1997) *Postmodern Fairy Tales: Gender and Narrative Strategies*, Philadelphia: University of Pennsylvania Press.

Bacchilega, C. and J. Rieder (2010) '"Mixing It Up": Generic Complexity and Gender Ideology in Early Twenty-First Century Fairy Tale Films', in P. Greenhill and S.E. Matrix (eds) *Fairy Tale Films: Visions of Ambiguity*, Logan: Utah State University Press.

Balio, T. (1987) *United Artists: The Company that Changed the Film Industry*, Madison: University of Wisconsin Press.

—— (1995) *Grand Design: Hollywood as a Modern Business Enterprise, 1930–1939*, Berkeley: University of California Press.

Barker, M. and E. Mathijs (eds) (2008) *Watching The Lord of the Rings: Tolkien's World Audiences*, New York: Peter Lang.

Barker, M., K. Egan, S. Jones and E. Mathijs (2008) 'Researching *The Lord of the Rings*: Audiences and Contexts', in M. Barker and E. Mathijs (eds) *Watching The Lord of the Rings: Tolkien's World Audiences*, New York: Peter Lang.

Barthes, R. (1990 [1970]) *S/Z*, trans. R. Miller, Oxford: Blackwell.

Bassil-Morozow, H. (2010) *Tim Burton: The Monster and the Crowd: A Post-Jungian Perspective*, London: Routledge.

Bazin, A. (2004 [1967]) *What is Cinema? Vol. 1*, trans. H. Gray, Berkeley: University of California Press.

Bell, E., L. Haas and L. Sells (eds) (1995) *From Mouse to Mermaid: The Politics of Film, Gender and Culture*, Bloomington: Indiana University Press.

Bellin, J.D. (2005) *Framing Monsters: Fantasy Film and Social Alienation*, Carbondale: Southern Illinois University Press.

Belton, J. (1992) *Widescreen Cinema*, Cambridge: Harvard University Press.

—— (1996) 'Technology and Innovation', in G. Nowell-Smith (ed.) *The Oxford History of World Cinema*, Oxford: Oxford University Press.

Benshoff, H. (1997) *Monsters in the Closet: Homosexuality and the Horror Film*, Manchester: Manchester University Press.

Benshoff, H. and S. Griffin (2009) *America on Film: Representing Race, Class, Gender, and Sexuality at the Movies*, Second Edition, Oxford: Wiley-Blackwell.

Berger, Richard (2008) '"Are There Any More at Home Like You?": Rewiring Superman', *Journal of Adaptation in Film and Performance*, Vol.1 No.2, 87–101.

Bettelheim, B. (1991 [1976]) *The Uses of Enchantment: The Meaning and Importance of Fairy Tales*, London: Penguin Books.

Bolter, J.D. and R. Grusin (1999) *Remediation: Understanding New Media*, Cambridge: MIT Press.

Booker, C. (2004) *The Seven Basic Plots: Why We Tell Stories*, London: Continuum.

Bordwell, D. (1985) *Narration in the Fiction Film*, London: Methuen.

—— (2006) *The Way Hollywood Tells It: Story and Style in Modern Movies*, Berkeley: University of California Press.

Bordwell, D. and K. Thompson (2004) *Film Art: An Introduction*, Seventh Edition, London and New York: McGraw-Hill.

Bordwell, D., J. Staiger and K. Thompson (1985) *The Classical Hollywood Cinema: Film Style and Mode of Production to 1960*, London: Routledge.

Bowles, S. (2008) 'Is *The Dark Knight* Too Dark for Kids?', *USA Today*, 21 July. Available online: <http://www.usatoday.com/life/movies/news/2008-07-20-dark-knight-no-kids_N.htm> (accessed 5 February 2011).

Brooker, W. (1999) 'Batman: One Life, Many Faces', in D. Cartmell and I. Whelehan (eds) *Adaptations: From Text to Screen, Screen to Text*, London: Routledge.

Buscombe, E. (1985) 'Sound and Colour', in B. Nichols (ed.) *Movies and Methods, Volume II*, Berkeley: University of California Press.

Butler, D. (2009) *Fantasy Cinema: Impossible Worlds on Screen*, London: Wallflower Press.

Campbell, J. (1993 [1949]) *The Hero with a Thousand Faces*, London: Fontana Press.

Carroll, L. (2010 [1865; 1871]) *Alice's Adventures in Wonderland and Through the Looking Glass*, New York: Cosimo Classics.

Carter, A. (ed.) (1990) *The Old Wives' Fairy Tale Book*, New York: Pantheon.

—— (1993 [1979]) *The Sadeian Woman and the Ideology of Pornography*, New York: Pantheon.

—— (2008) 'Afterword', in *The Fairy Tales of Charles Perrault*, trans. A. Carter, London: Penguin.

Carter, C. and C.K. Weaver (2003) *Violence and the Media*, Buckingham: Open University Press.

Cartmell, D. (2007) 'Adapting Children's Literature', in D. Cartmell and I. Whelehan (eds) *The Cambridge Companion to Literature on Screen*, Cambridge: Cambridge University Press.

Cartmell, D. and I. Whelehan (2005) 'Harry Potter and the Fidelity Debate', in M. Aragay (ed.) *Books in Motion, Adaptation, Intertextuality, Authorship*, Amsterdam and New York: Rodopi.

Chance, J. (2001) *The Lord of the Rings: The Mythology of Power*, Lexington: Kentucky University Press.

Cherry, B. (2009) *Horror*, London: Routledge.

Christie, I. (1994) *The Last Machine: Early Cinema and the Birth of the Modern World*, London: BFI.

Clark, K. (2010) 'Interview: Tim Burton for *Alice in Wonderland*', *ScreenCrave*, 4 March. Available online: <http://screencrave.com/2010-03-04/interview-tim-burton-for-alice-in-wonderland/> (accessed 22 January 2011).

Clute, J. and J. Grant (1997) *The Encyclopedia of Fantasy*, London: Orbit.

Collins, R. and H. Pearce (eds) (1985) *The Scope of the Fantastic: Theory, Technique, Major Authors*, Westport: Greenwood Press.

Cook, D.A. (2002) *Lost Illusions: American Cinema in the Shadow of Watergate and Vietnam, 1970–1979*, Berkeley: University of California Press.

Coombs, N. (2007) *Studying Surrealist and Fantasy Cinema*, Leighton Buzzard: Auteur Publishing.

Cowie, E. (1993) 'From Fantasia', in A. Easthope (ed.) *Contemporary Film Theory*, London: Longman.

Crandall, N. (2006) 'The Fairy Tale in the 21st Century: *Shrek* as Anticipatory Illumination or Coercive Ideology', in F.M. Collins and J. Ridgman (eds) *Turning the Page: Children's Literature in Performance and the Media*, Bern: Peter Lang.

Creed, B. (2003) *Media Matrix: Sexing the New Reality*, Crows Nest, NSW: Allen & Unwin.

—— (2007) 'The Untamed Eye and the Dark Side of Surrealism: Hitchcock, Lynch and Cronenberg', in G. Harper and R. Stone (eds) *The Unsilvered Screen: Surrealism on Film*, London: Wallflower Press.

Crowther, B. (1946) '*It's a Wonderful Life*', *The New York Times*, 23 December, 19.

Davis, R.B. (ed.) (2010) *Alice in Wonderland and Philosophy: Curiouser and Curiouser*, New Jersey: John Wiley and Sons.

Dawson, J. (2008) 'Has the New Batman Plundered Its Plot from 9/11?', *The Sunday Times*, 20 July. Available online: <http://entertainment.times online.co.uk/tol/arts_and_entertainment/film/article4352512.ece> (accessed 5 February 2011).

Day, A. (1998) *Angela Carter: The Rational Glass*, Manchester: Manchester University Press.

Denison, R. (2004) 'Film Reviews: *Pirates of the Caribbean: The Curse of the Black Pearl*', *Scope*, November. Available online: <http://www.scope.nottingham.ac.uk/filmreview.php?issue=nov2004&id=675&section=film_rev> (accessed 5 February 2011).

Devlin, W. (2008) 'Some Paradoxes of Time Travel in *The Terminator* and *Twelve Monkeys*', in S. Sanders (ed.) *The Philosophy of Science Fiction Film*, Lexington: University Press of Kentucky.

Donald, J. (ed.) (1989) *Fantasy and the Cinema*, London: BFI.

Donnelly, K. (2006) 'Musical Middle Earth', in E. Mathijs (ed.) *The Lord of the Rings: Popular Culture in Global Context*, London: Wallflower Press.

Duncan Smith, I. (2008) 'Batman Film Rating Is Not Right for Children', *The Times*, 5 August, 23.

Dundes, A. (2009) 'Introduction to the Second Edition', in V. Propp, *Morphology of the Folktale*, trans. L. Scott, Second Edition, Austin: University of Texas Press.

Dyer, R. (2002) 'Entertainment and Utopia', in *Only Entertainment*, Second Edition, London: Routledge.

Easthope, A. (ed.) (1993) *Contemporary Film Theory*, London: Longman.

Eliade, M. (1963) *Myth and Reality*, trans. W.R. Trask, New York: Harper and Row.

—— (1974) *Shamanism: Archaic Techniques of Ecstasy*, trans. W.R. Trask, Princeton: Princeton University Press.

Elsaesser, T. (1996) 'Germany: The Weimar Years', in G. Nowell-Smith (ed.) *The Oxford History of World Cinema*, Oxford: Oxford University Press.

Erens, P. (1990) *Issues in Feminist Film Criticism*, Bloomington: Indiana University Press.

Felperin, L. (2006) 'Reviews: Films: *Pirates of the Caribbean: Dead Man's Chest*', *Sight and Sound*, 16:9 September, 65–6.

Fhlainn, S.N. (ed.) (2010) *The Worlds of Back to the Future: Critical Essays on the Films*, Jefferson: McFarland.

Fiske, J. (1987) *Television Culture*, London: Methuen.

Fowkes, K. (2010) *The Fantasy Film*, Oxford: Wiley-Blackwell.

Freud, S. (1990) *Art and Literature*, Vol.14, trans. J. Strachey, Harmondsworth: Penguin.

—— (1991) *The Interpretation of Dreams*, Vol.4, trans. J. Strachey, Harmondsworth: Penguin.

Friedman, L.D. (2006) *Citizen Spielberg*, Urbana: University of Illinois Press.

Friedman, T. (2009) 'The Politics of Magic: Fantasy Media, Technology, and Nature in the 21st Century', *Scope*, Issue 14, June. Available online: <http://www.scope.nottingham.ac.uk/article.php?issue=14&id=1138> (accessed 5 February 2011).

Furby, J. (2005) 'Rhizomatic Time and Temporal Poetics in *American Beauty*', in J. Furby and K. Randell (eds) *Screen Methods: Comparative Readings in Film Studies*, London: Wallflower Press.

Geraghty, C. (2008) *Now a Major Motion Picture: Film Adaptations of Literature and Drama*, Lanham: Rowman and Littlefield.

Giannetti, L. (2005) *Understanding Movies*, Tenth Edition, New Jersey: Pearson Education.

Gordon, A. (2004) '*Back to the Future*: Oedipus as Time Traveller', in S. Redmond (ed.) *Liquid Metal: The Science Fiction Film Reader*, London: Wallflower Press.

—— (2008) *Empire of Dreams: The Science Fiction and Fantasy Films of Seven Spielberg*, Lanham: Rowman & Littlefield.

Grainge, P. (2008) *Brand Hollywood: Selling Entertainment in a Global Media Age*, London: Routledge.

Grant, B.K. (ed.) (1986) *Film Genre Reader*, Austin: University of Texas Press.

Greene, E. (1998) *Planet of the Apes as American Myth: Race, Politics, and Popular Culture*, Second Edition, Middletown: Wesleyan University Press.

Grimm, J. and W. Grimm (2005) *Selected Tales*, trans. J. Crick, Oxford: Oxford University Press.

Grosz, E. (1990) *Jacques Lacan: A Feminist Introduction*, London: Routledge.

Grundmann, U. and R. Arnheim (2001) 'The Intelligence of Vision: An Interview with Rudolf Arnheim', *Cabinet: Mapping Conversations*, Issue 2, Spring. Available online: <http://www.cabinetmagazine.org/issues/2/rudolfarnheim.php> (accessed 5 February 2011).

Guerrero, E. (1993) *Framing Blackness: The African American Image in Film*, Philadelphia: Temples University Press.

Gunning, T. (1990) 'The Cinema of Attractions: Early Film, Its Spectator and the Avant-Garde', in T. Elsaesser (ed.) *Early Cinema: Space, Frame, Narrative*, London: BFI.

—— (1995) 'Colorful Metaphors: The Attraction of Color in Early Silent Cinema', *Fotogenia*, No.1. Available online: <http://www.muspe.unibo.it/period/fotogen/num01/numero1d.htm> (accessed 5 February 2011).

Haase, D. (ed.) (2004) *Fairy Tales and Feminism: New Approaches*, Detroit: Wayne State University Press.

—— (ed.) (2008) *The Greenwood Encyclopedia of Folktales and Fairy Tales*, Westport: Greenwood Press.

Hayward, S. (2000) *Cinema Studies: The Key Concepts*, Second Edition, London: Routledge.

Henderson, J. (1964) 'Ancient Myths and Modern Man', in C. Jung (ed.) *Man and His Symbols*, London: Picador.

Higgins, S. (2007) *Harnessing the Technicolor Rainbow: Color Design in the 1930s*, Austin: University of Texas Press.

Hockley, L. (2001) *Cinematic Projections: The Analytical Psychology of C.G. Jung and Film Theory*, Luton: University of Luton Press.

Hume, K. (1984) *Fantasy and Mimesis: Response to Reality in Western Literature*, New York: Methuen.

Hunter, I. (2007) 'Post-classical Fantasy Cinema: The Lord of the Rings', in D. Cartmell and I. Whelehan (eds) *The Cambridge Companion to Literature on Screen*, Cambridge: Cambridge University Press.

Hutcheon, L. (2006) *A Theory of Adaptation*, London: Routledge.

Iaccino, J.F. (1998) *Jungian Reflections within the Cinema: A Psychological Analysis of Sci-Fi and Fantasy Archetypes*, Westport: Praeger.

Inness, S. (1999) *Tough Girls: Women Warriors and Wonder Women in Popular Culture*, Philadelphia: University of Pennsylvania Press.

Jackson, R. (1998) *Fantasy: The Literature of Subversion*, London: Routledge.

Jenkins, H. (2006) *Convergence Culture: Where Old and New Media Collide*, New York: New York University Press.

Jesse-Cooke, C. (2010) 'Sequalizing Spectatorship and Building Up the Kingdom: The Case of *Pirates of the Caribbean*, Or, How a Theme-Park Attraction Spawned a Multibillion-Dollar Film Franchise', in C. Jesse-Cooke and C. Verevis (eds) *Second Takes: Critical Approaches to the Film Sequel*, Albany: State University of New York Press.

Jung, C. (1964) 'Approaching the Unconscious', in C. Jung (ed.) *Man and His Symbols*, London: Picador.

—— (2010 [1959]) *The Archetypes and the Collective Unconscious*, Vol.9 Part 1, trans. R.F. Hull, London: Routledge.

Kaplan, E.A. (ed.) (2000) *Feminism and Film*, Oxford: Oxford University Press.

Keane, S. (2007) *CineTech: Film, Convergence and New Media*, Basingstoke: Palgrave Macmillan.

Kellner, D. (2006) '*The Lord of the Rings* as Allegory: A Multiperspectivist Reading', in E. Mathijs and M. Pomerance (eds) *From Hobbits to Hollywood: Essays on Peter Jackson's Lord of the Rings*, New York: Rodopi.

Kim, S.J. (2009) 'The Business of Race in *The Lord of the Rings* Trilogy', in R. Sickels (ed.) *The Business of Entertainment: Movies*, Westport: Greenwood Press.

King, G. (2000) *Spectacular Narratives: Hollywood in the Age of the Blockbuster*, London: I.B. Tauris.

—— (2006) 'Spectacle and Narrative in the Contemporary Blockbuster', in L.R. Williams and M. Hammond (eds) *Contemporary American Cinema*, London: Open University Press.

King, G. and T. Krzywinska (eds) (2002) *ScreenPlay: cinema/videogames/interfaces*, London: Wallflower Press.

Klinger, B. (2006a) *Beyond the Multiplex: Cinema, New Technologies and the Home*, Berkeley: University of California Press.

—— (2006b) 'What is Cinema Today? Home Viewing, New Technologies on DVD', in L.R. Williams and M. Hammond (eds) *Contemporary American Cinema*, London: Open University Press.

Kracauer, S. (1997 [1960]) Theory of Film: The Redemption of Physical Reality, Princeton: Princeton University Press.

—— (2004 [1960]) 'Basic Concepts', in L. Braudy and M. Cohen (eds) Film Theory and Criticism: Introductory Readings, Sixth Edition, Oxford: Oxford University Press.

Krämer, P. (2005) The New Hollywood: From Bonnie and Clyde to Star Wars, London: Wallflower Press.

Krzywinska, T. (2008) 'World Creation and Lore: World of Warcraft as Rich Text', in H.G. Corneliussen and J. Walker Rettberg (eds) Digital Culture, Play, and Identity: A World of Warcraft Reader, Cambridge: MIT Press.

Lacan, J. (2001) Écrits: A Selection, trans. A. Sheridan, London: Routledge.

Langford, B. (2005) Film Genre: Hollywood and Beyond, Edinburgh: Edinburgh University Press.

Laplanche, J. and J.-B. Pontalis (1986) 'Fantasy and the Origins of Sexuality', in V. Burgin, J. Donald and C. Kaplan (eds) Formations of Fantasy, London: Methuen.

—— (2006 [1973]) The Language of Psycho-Analysis, London: Karnac Books.

Leitch, T. (2007) Film Adaptation and Its Discontents: From Gone with the Wind to The Passion of the Christ, Baltimore: The Johns Hopkins University Press.

Levin, R. (1990) 'Psychoanalytic Theories on the Function of Dreams: A Review of the Empirical Dream Research', in J. Masling (ed.) Empirical Studies of Psychoanalytic Theories, Vol. 3, Hillsdale: Analytic Press.

Lévi-Strauss, C. (1969) The Raw and the Cooked, trans. J. Weightman and D. Weightman, Chicago: University of Chicago Press.

—— (1978) Myth and Meaning, London: Routledge.

Lim, B.C. (2005) 'Serial Time: Bluebeard in Stepford', in R. Stam and A. Raengo (eds) Literature and Film: A Guide to the Theory and Practice of Film Adaptation, Oxford: Blackwell.

Lucas, J.R. (2009) 'Determinism', in R. Fumerton and D. Jeske (eds) Introducing Philosophy Through Film: Key Texts, Discussion, and Film Selections, Oxford: Blackwell.

McCartney, J. (2008) 'The Dark Knight Taints Our Children's World View', The Telegraph, 26 July. Available online: <http://www.telegraph.co.uk/comment/columnists/charlesmoore/3560989/The-Dark-Knight-taints-our-childrens-world-view.html> (accessed 5 February 2011).

McFarlane, B. (1996) Novel to Film: An Introduction to the Theory of Adaptation, Oxford: Clarendon Press.

McGavin, P. (2008) 'Journey to the Third Dimension', *Screen International*, 1 August, 22–3.

Mackey-Kallis, S. (2001) *The Hero and the Perennial Journey Home in American Film*, Philadelphia: University of Pennsylvania Press.

Maltby, R. (2003) *Hollywood Cinema*, Second Edition, Oxford: Blackwell.

Markley, R. (2007) 'Geek/Goth: Remediation and Nostalgia in Tim Burton's *Edward Scissorhands*', in L.M.E. Goodlad and M. Bibby (eds) *Goth: Undead Subculture*, Durham: Duke University Press.

Matthews, R. (2002) *Fantasy: The Liberation of Imagination*, New York and London: Routledge.

Metz, C. (1982) *Psychoanalysis and Cinema: The Imaginary Signifier*, trans. C Britton, A. Williams, B. Brewster and A. Guzzetti, London: Macmillan.

Mitchell, C.A. and J. Reid-Walsh (eds) (2008) *Girl Culture: An Encyclopedia*, Westport: Greenwood Press.

Morton, R. (2005) *King Kong: the History of a Movie Icon from Fay Wray to Peter Jackson*, New York: Applause Books.

Mulvey, L. (1989) 'Visual Pleasure and Narrative Cinema', in *Visual and Other Pleasures*, London: Macmillan.

Munby, J. (2000) 'A Hollywood Carol's Wonderful Life', in M. Connelly (ed.) *Christmas at the Movies: Images of Christmas in American, British and European Cinema*, London: I.B. Tauris.

Napier, S. (2005) *Anime from Akira to Howl's Moving Castle*, Updated Edition, Basingstoke: Palgrave Macmillan.

Ndalianis, A. (2000) 'Special Effects, Morphing Magic, and the 1990s Cinema of Attractions', in V. Sobchack (ed.) *Meta-Morphing: Visual Transformation and the Culture of Quick Change*, Minneapolis: University of Minnesota Press.

Neale, S. (1980) *Genre*, London: BFI.

—— (1995) 'Questions of Genre', in O. Boyd-Barrett and C. Newbold (eds) *Approaches to Media: A Reader*, London: Arnold.

—— (2000) *Genre and Hollywood*, London: Routledge.

—— (2006) 'Technicolor', in A. Vacche and B. Price (eds) *Color: The Film Reader*, London: Routledge.

Nel, P. (2009) 'Lost in Translation? Harry Potter, from Page to Screen', in E.E. Heilman (ed.) *Critical Perspectives on Harry Potter*, New York and Abingdon: Routledge.

Nichols, B. (2001) *Introduction to Documentary*, Bloomington: Indiana University Press.

—— (2010) *Engaging Cinema: An Introduction to Film Studies*, New York: Norton.

North, D. (2008) *Performing Illusions: Cinema, Special Effects and the Virtual Actor*, London: Wallflower Press.

O'Shaughnessy, M. and J. Stadler (2002) *Media and Society: An Introduction*, Second Edition, Oxford: Oxford University Press.

Pearson, A. (2008) 'Holy Cretins, Batman, This Is No Family Film', *Mail Online*, 30 July. Available online: <http://www.dailymail.co.uk/news/article-1039729/ALLISON-PEARSON-Holy-cretins-Batman-family-film.html#ixzz1364zezJY> (accessed 5 February 2011).

Penley, C. (1996) 'Time Travel, Primal Scene and the Critical Dystopia', in A. Kuhn (ed.) *Alien Zone: Cultural Theory and Contemporary Science Fiction Cinema*, London and New York: Verso.

Petersen, A.H. (2009) '"You believe in pirates, of course . . .": Disney's Commodification and "Closure" of Pirates of the Caribbean', in R. Sickels (ed.) *The Business of Entertainment: Movies*, Westport: Greenwood Press.

Petrie, D. (ed.) (1993) *Cinema and the Realms of Enchantment*, London: BFI.

Pierson, M. (2002) *Special Effects: Still in Search of Wonder*, New York: Columbia University Press.

Pisters, P. (2003) *The Matrix of Visual Culture: Working with Deleuze in Film Theory*, Stanford: Stanford University Press.

Popple, S. and J. Kember (2004) *Early Cinema: From Factory Gate to Dream Factory*, London: Wallflower Press.

Pratchett, T., I. Stewart, and J.S. Cohen (2002) *The Science of Discworld II: The Globe*, London: Ebury Press.

Pringle, D. (ed.) (1998) *The Ultimate Encyclopedia of Fantasy*, Woodstock: Overlook Press.

Propp, V. (2009) *Morphology of the Folktale*, trans. L. Scott, Second Edition, Austin: University of Texas Press.

Pye, M. and L. Miles (1999) 'George Lucas', in S. Kline (ed.) *George Lucas: Interview*, Jackson: University Press of Mississippi.

Ragland-Sullivan, E. (1986) *Jacques Lacan and the Philosophy of Psychoanalysis*, Urbana and Chicago: University of Illinois Press.

—— (1992) 'Lacan, Jacques', in E. Wright (ed.) *Feminism and Psychoanalysis: A Critical Dictionary*, Oxford: Blackwell.

Redmond, S. (2008) 'The Whiteness of the Rings', in D. Bernardi (ed.) *The Persistence of Whiteness: Race and Contemporary Hollywood Cinema*, London: Routledge.

Richards, J. (1977) *Swordsmen of the Screen: From Douglas Fairbanks to Michael York*, London: Routledge.

Richardson, M. (2006) *Surrealism and Cinema*, Oxford: Berg.

Robinson, D. (1993) *Georges Méliès: Father of Film Fantasy*, London: BFI.

Roddick, N. (2006) 'Rushes: Mr Busy: Helium Buccaneers', *Sight and Sound*, 16:11 November, 10.

Ryan, M. and D. Kellner (1990) *Camera Politica: The Politics and Ideology of Contemporary Hollywood Film*, Bloomington: Indiana University Press.

The St Louis Court Brief (2003 [2002]) 'Debating Audience "Effects" in Public', *Particip@tions*, 1:1 November. Available online: <http://www.participations. org/volume%201/issue%201/1_01_amici_contents.htm> (accessed 5 February 2011).

Salisbury, M. (ed.) (2000) *Burton on Burton*, Revised Edition, London: Faber and Faber.

Sanders, J. (2006) *Adaptation and Appropriation*, London: Routledge.

Saussure, F. de (1983 [1916]) *Course in General Linguistics*, trans. R. Harris, Illinois: Open Court.

Schatz, T. (1999) *Boom and Bust: American Cinema in the 1940s*, Berkeley: University of California Press.

—— (2003) 'The Structural Influence: New Directions in Film Genre Study', in B.K. Grant (ed.) *Film Genre Reader III*, Austin: University of Texas Press.

Sergi, G. (2004) *The Dolby Era: Film Sound in Contemporary Hollywood*, Manchester: Manchester University Press.

Shippey, T. (2004) 'Another Road to Middle Earth: Jackson's Movie Trilogy', in R.A. Zimbardo and N.D. Isaacs (eds) *Understanding The Lord of the Rings: The Best of Tolkien Criticism*, New York: Houghton Mifflin.

Simmons, J. (2005) 'Harry Potter, Marketing Magician', *The Observer*, 6 June. Available online: <http://www.guardian.co.uk/business/2005/jun/ 26/media.books> (accessed 5 February 2011).

Sobchack, V. (1996) 'The Fantastic', in G. Nowell-Smith (ed.) *The Oxford History of World Cinema*, Oxford: Oxford University Press.

Staiger, J. (2003) 'Hybrid or Inbred: The Purity Hypothesis and Hollywood Genre History', in B.K. Grant (ed.) *Film Genre Reader III*, Austin: University of Texas Press.

Stam, R. (2000) *Film Theory: An Introduction*, Oxford: Blackwell.

—— (2005a) *Literature Through Film: Realism, Magic, and the Art of Adaptation*, Malden and Oxford: Blackwell.

—— (2005b) 'Introduction: The Theory and Practice of Adaptation', in R. Stam and A. Raengo (eds) *Literature and Film: A Guide to the Theory and Practice of Adaptation*, Malden and Oxford: Blackwell.

Staples, T. (2008) 'The Brothers Grimm in Biopics', in D. Haase (ed.) *The Greenwood Encyclopedia of Folktales and Fairy Tales*, Westport: Greenwood Press.

Steiner, R. (ed.) (2003) *Unconscious Phantasy*, London. Karnac Books.

Tasker, Y. (1993) *Spectacular Bodies: Gender, Genre and the Action Cinema*, London: Routledge.

—— (1998) *Working Girls: Gender and Sexuality in Popular Cinema*, London: Routledge.

Taves, B. (1993) *The Romance of Adventure: The Genre of Historical Adventure Movies*, Jackson: University Press of Mississippi.

Telotte, J.P. (2001) *Science Fiction Film*, Cambridge: Cambridge University Press.

Thompson, K. (2003) 'Fantasy, Franchises, and Frodo Baggins: *The Lord of the Rings* and Modern Hollywood', *The Velvet Light Trap*, 52, 45–63.

—— (2008a) 'Digital Grading and the Colours of Middle Earth', *Kristin Thompson's weblog*, 28 February. Available online: <http://www.kristinthompson.net/blog/?p=195> (accessed 5 February 2011).

—— (2008b) *The Frodo Franchise: The Lord of the Rings and Modern Hollywood*, Berkeley: University of California Press.

Thornham, S. (1997) *Passionate Detachments: An Introduction to Feminist Film Theory*, London: Arnold.

Todorov, T. (1975) *The Fantastic: A Structural Approach to a Literary Genre*, trans. R. Howard, Ithaca: Cornell University Press.

—— (1977) *The Poetics of Prose*, trans. R. Howard, Ithaca: Cornell University Press.

Tolkien, J.R.R. (1966) 'On Fairy-stories', in *The Tolkien Reader*, New York: Random House.

Thwaites, T., L. Davis and W. Mules (1994) *Tools for Cultural Studies: An Introduction*, South Melbourne: Macmillan.

Trend, D. (2007) *The Myth of Media Violence: A Critical Introduction*, Oxford: Blackwell.

Turner, G. (2006) *Film as Social Practice*, Fourth Edition, London: Routledge.

Valenti, P.L. (1978) 'The "Film Blanc": Suggestions for a Variety of Fantasy, 1940–45', *Journal of Popular Film*, Vol.VI No.4, 294–304.

—— (2003) 'The Cultural Hero in the World War II Fantasy Film', in W.L. Hixson (ed.) *The American Experience in World War II: The United States and the Road to War in Europe Vol.1*, London: Routledge.

Vogler, C. (2007) *The Writer's Journey: Mythic Structure for Writers*, Third Edition, Studio City: Michael Wiese Productions.

Von Gunden, K. (1989) *Flights of Fancy: The Great Fantasy Films*, Jefferson: McFarland.

Warner, M. (1992) 'Angela Carter', *The Independent*, 17 February, 25.

—— (1995) *From the Beast to the Blonde: On Fairy Tales and Their Tellers*, London: Vintage.

—— (2006) *Phantasmagoria*, Oxford: Oxford University Press.

Wasko, J. (2001) *Understanding Disney: The Manufacture of Fantasy*, Cambridge: Polity Press.

—— (2008) 'The Lord of the Rings: Selling the Franchise', in M. Barker and E. Mathijs (eds) *Watching The Lord of the Rings: Tolkien's World Audiences*, New York: Peter Lang.

Watson, P. (2003) 'Critical Approaches to Hollywood Cinema: Authorship, Genre, and Stars', in J. Nelmes (ed.) *An Introduction to Film Studies*, Third Edition, London: Routledge.

Wells, P. (1998) *Understanding Animation*, London and New York: Routledge.

—— (2002) *Animation: Genre and Authorship*, London: Wallflower Press.

Wood, A. (2002) *Technoscience in Contemporary American Film: Beyond Science Fiction*, Manchester: Manchester University Press.

Wood, R. (1986) *Hollywood from Vietnam to Reagan*, New York: Columbia University Press.

—— (2004) 'Ideology, Genre, Auteur', in L. Braudy and M. Cohen (eds) *Film Theory and Criticism: Introductory Readings*, Sixth Edition, Oxford: Oxford University Press.

Worley, A. (2005) *Empires of the Imagination: A Critical Survey of Fantasy Cinema from Georges Méliès to The Lord of the Rings*, Jefferson: McFarland.

Yatt, J. (2002) 'Wraiths and Race', *Guardian*, 2 December. Available online: <http://www.guardian.co.uk/books/2002/dec/02/jrrtolkien.lordofth erings> (accessed 5 February 2011).

Ziolkowski, J. (2009) *Fairy Tales from Before Fairy Tales: The Medieval Latin Past of Wonderful Lies*, Ann Arbor: University of Michigan Press.

Zipes, J. (1994) *Fairy Tale as Myth/Myth as Fairy Tale*, Lexington: University Press of Kentucky.

—— (2000) *The Oxford Companion to Fairy Tales: The Western Fairy Tale Tradition From Medieval to Modern*, Oxford: OUP.

—— (2002) *Breaking the Magic Spell: Radical Theories of Folk and Fairy Tales*, Revised and Expanded Edition, Lexington: University Press of Kentucky.

—— (2006a) *Fairy Tales and the Art of Subversion*, Second Edition, London: Routledge.

—— (2006b) *Why Fairy Tales Stick: The Evolution and Relevance of a Genre*, London: Routledge.

—— (2007) *When Dreams Came True: Classical Fairy Tales and their Tradition*, Second Edition, London: Routledge.

INDEX

www.routledge.com/media

Also in the Routledge Film Guidebooks Series

Routledge Film Guidebooks
Documentary

David Saunders

Dave Saunders' spirited introduction to documentary covers its history, cultural context and development, and the approaches, controversies and functions pertaining to non-fiction filmmaking. Saunders examines the many methods by which documentary conveys meaning, whilst exploring its differing societal purposes. From early, one-reel 'actualities' to the box-office successes of recent years, artistic complexities have been inherent to non-fiction cinema, and this *Guidebook* aims to make such issues clearer.

After a historical consideration of international documentary production, the author examines the impact of recent technological developments on the production, distribution and viewing of non-fiction. In addition, he explores the increasingly hazy distinctions between factual and dramatic formats, discussing 'reality television', the 'docu-drama', and less orthodox approaches including animated and fantastical representations of reality.

Documentary encompasses a broad range of academic discourse around non-fiction filmmaking, introducing readers to the key filmmakers, major scholars, central debates and critical ideas relating to the form. This wide-ranging guidebook features global releases from the 1920s through to 2009.

Hb: 978-0-415-47309-5
Pb: 978-0-415-47310-1
eBook: 978-0-203-85268-2

For more information and to order a copy visit
www.routledge.com/9780415473101

Available from all good bookshops

www.routledge.com/media

ROUTLEDGE

Also in the Routledge Film Guidebooks Series

Routledge Film Guidebooks
Romantic Comedy

Claire Mortimer

Romantic comedy is an enduringly popular genre which has maintained its appeal by constantly evolving, from the screwball comedy to the recent emergence of the bromance.

Romantic Comedy examines the history of the genre, considering the social and cultural context for key developments in new genre cycles. It studies the key themes and issues at work within romantic comedy films, focusing in particular on the representation of gender and how the genre acts as a barometer for gender politics in the course of the twentieth century.

Claire Mortimer provides the reader with a comprehensive overview of the genre, tracing its development, enduring appeal, stars and the nature of its comedy. Mortimer discusses both British and Hollywood with in-depth case studies spanning a wide variety of films, including:

- It Happened One Night
- Bringing Up Baby
- Annie Hall
- Four Weddings and a Funeral
- Bridget Jones's Diary
- Wimbledon
- Knocked Up
- Sex and the City

This book is the perfect introduction to the romantic comedy genre and will be particularly useful for all those investigating this area within film, media or women's studies.

Hb: 978-0-415-54862-5
Pb: 978-0-415-54863-2
eBook: 978-0-203-85143-2

For more information and to order a copy visit
www.routledge.com/9780415548632

Available from all good bookshops

www.routledge.com/media

Also in the Routledge Film Guidebooks Series

Routledge Film Guidebooks
Horror

Cherry Brigid

Horror cinema is a hugely successful, but at the same time culturally illicit genre that spans the history of cinema. It continues to flourish with recent cycles of supernatural horror and torture porn that span the full range of horror styles and aesthetics. It is enjoyed by audiences everywhere, but also seen as a malign influence by others.

In this Routledge Film Guidebook, audience researcher and film scholar Brigid Cherry provides a comprehensive overview of the horror film and explores how the genre works. Examining the way horror films create images of gore and the uncanny through film technology and effects, Cherry provides an account of the way cinematic and stylistic devices create responses of terror and disgust in the viewer.

Horror examines the way these films construct psychological and cognitive responses and how they speak to audiences on an intimate personal level, addressing their innermost fears and desires. Cherry further explores the role of horror cinema in society and culture, looking at how it represents various identity groups and engages with social anxieties, and examining the way horror sees, and is seen by, society.

Hb: 978-0-415-45667-8
Pb: 978-0-415-45668-5
eBook: 978-0-203-88218-4

For more information and to order a copy visit
www.routledge.com/9780415456685

Available from all good bookshops

Taylor & Francis

eBooks

FOR LIBRARIES

ORDER YOUR
FREE 30 DAY
INSTITUTIONAL
TRIAL TODAY!

Over 23,000 eBook titles in the Humanities,
Social Sciences, STM and Law from some of the
world's leading imprints.

Choose from a range of subject packages or create your own!

Benefits for
you

▶ Free MARC records
▶ COUNTER-compliant usage statistics
▶ Flexible purchase and pricing options

Benefits
for your
user

▶ Off-site, anytime access via Athens or referring URL
▶ Print or copy pages or chapters
▶ Full content search
▶ Bookmark, highlight and annotate text
▶ Access to thousands of pages of quality research
at the click of a button

For more information, pricing enquiries or to order
a free trial, contact your local online sales team.

UK and Rest of World: **online.sales@tandf.co.uk**

US, Canada and Latin America:
e-reference@taylorandfrancis.com

www.ebooksubscriptions.com

ALPSP Award for
BEST eBOOK
PUBLISHER
2009 Finalist

Taylor & Francis **eBooks**
Taylor & Francis Group

A flexible and dynamic resource for teaching, learning and research.